Sing a Rhythm, Dance a Blues

Also by Monique W. Morris

Pushout: The Criminalization of Black Girls in Schools

Black Stats: African Americans by the Numbers in the Twenty-First Century

Too Beautiful for Words: A Novel

SING A RHYTHM, DANCE A BLUES

EDUCATION FOR THE LIBERATION OF
BLACK AND BROWN GIRLS

Monique W. Morris

THE
NEW
PRESS

NEW YORK
LONDON

Grateful acknowledgement is made to Hal Leonard LLC for permission to use lyrics from the songs "I'm a Woman" performed by Koko Taylor, "Young Woman's Blues" performed by Bessie Smith, and "Cell Bound Blues" performed by Gertrude "Ma" Rainey; Alfred Music for permission to use lyrics from the songs "You Let Me Down" performed by Billie Holiday and "God Bless the Child" performed by Billie Holiday; and Simon & Schuster for permission to use lines from *For Colored Girls Who Have Considered Suicide When the Rainbow Is Enuf* by Ntozake Shange.

Published in the United States by The New Press, New York, 2019
Distributed by Two Rivers Distribution

ISBN 978-1-62097-399-8 (hc)
ISBN 978-1-62097-400-1 (ebook)
CIP data is available

The New Press publishes books that promote and enrich public discussion and understanding of the issues vital to our democracy and to a more equitable world. These books are made possible by the enthusiasm of our readers; the support of a committed group of donors, large and small; the collaboration of our many partners in the independent media and the not-for-profit sector; booksellers, who often hand-sell New Press books; librarians; and above all by our authors.

www.thenewpress.com

Funding generously provided by the Art for Justice Fund, a sponsored project of Rockefeller Philanthropy Advisors.

ART FOR JUSTICE FUND

Book design and composition by Bookbright Media
This book was set in Minion Pro and Avenir Next

Printed in the United States of America

2 4 6 8 10 9 7 5 3 1

For Black and Brown girls—
and the people who cherish them

Schools can therefore be seen as the most powerful alternative to jails and prisons. Unless the current structures of violence are eliminated from schools in impoverished communities of color—including the presence of armed security guards and police—and unless schools become places that encourage the joy of learning, these schools will remain the major conduits to prisons. The alternative would be to transform schools into vehicles for decarceration.

—Angela Y. Davis

Contents

Prelude

Everything, everything, everything gon' be alright,
Oh yeah.

When I was a little girl,
Only twelve years old,
I couldn't do nothing
To save my dog-gone soul.
My mama told me
The day I was grown,
She says, "Sing the blues, child,
Sing it from now on."

I'm a woman, oh yeah.
I'm a woman, I'm a ball of fire.
I'm a woman, I can make love to a crocodile.
I'm a woman, I can sing the blues.
I'm a woman, I can change old to new.
Spelled w-o-m-a-n.

—Ellas McDaniel (Bo Diddley) and Koko Taylor, "I'm a
Woman" (Alligator Records, 1978)

Introduction

Blue Moments

somebody/anybody
sing a black girl's song
bring her out
to know herself
to know you
but sing her rhythms
carin/struggle/hard times
sing her song of life
      —*Ntozake Shange, "Dark Phrases,"* For Colored
      Girls Who Have Considered Suicide When the
      Rainbow Is Enuf

Oakland, California, July 2018.
    In the distance, we can hear a woman wail a gut-wrenching cry that sings of a trauma so severe, all of us can feel its effects. It pierces our souls. Her cry, while heartbreaking, is melodic. Her public display of grief is both intriguing and healing.

"That's my baby girl up there," Ansar Muhammad said to

a local news reporter.[1] The shock and sorrow in his eyes were paralyzing.

He was speaking of his daughter, eighteen-year-old Nia Wilson, who, along with her sister Lehtifa, was stabbed in an act of unprovoked hate by John Cowell on a BART train one night. Lehtifa suffered serious injuries to the neck. She survived, but her sister did not.

"I want justice for my daughter," her father said.

Justice for Nia. Her name means "purpose" in Swahili.

Justice for Lehtifa. Her name means "gentle" in Arabic.

Justice for girls who are the targets of violence, physical and otherwise. Justice for their purpose, justice for their gentle futures. The fatal stabbing of Nia Wilson, a high school student, occurred at the intersection between racism and gender-based violence, neither of which is random or unintended.

This volatile intersection leaves Black girls relatively unprotected from the *pattern* of violence that they experience in public and in private at the hands of strangers and those they love. This vulnerability opens a door for others to treat their marginalization as a creation of Black girls' own making, their truths obscured as entertainment.

Following her death, people of the Oakland community cried for Nia. They danced for her. They mourned her through altars and chants of "Say her name."[2]

We all sang a blues.

⌢

A grainy, black-and-white video of Billie Holiday singing "Strange Fruit" offers a meditation on the redemptive potential of the blues. In the video, Ms. Holiday stands in a glittery sweater dress, alone in the frame as a singular point of interest in the narrative about the heinous violence that surrounded her. Her long black hair is pulled into a ponytail, earrings dangle delicately beside her neck, falling just above her shoulders. Her interpretation of this blues classic that emerged from a lynching protest poem penned by Abel Meeropol was as fragile as Black America's grasp on justice. But it was also resilient. It was not just the words; it was her physical reading, her attitude while singing, that bestowed the greatest gifts.

> Southern trees bear strange fruit
> (*She wrinkles her brow and slightly frowns as her lips*
> *form the words.*)
> Black bodies swinging . . .
> (*She cocks her head, and then lingers in a distant stare.*)
> Here is fruit for the crows to pluck
> (*She blinks slowly and leans forward slightly while main-*
> *taining a frown.*)

Nia Wilson's body joined the panoply of strange fruit that unfortunately shape our memory and understanding of just how much Black lives matter in our racialized nation.

It's all so instructive. Upsetting. Liberating.

Angela Davis once described "Strange Fruit" as one of "the most influential and profound examples—and continuing sites—of the intersection of music and social consciousness. . . . By disrupting the landscape of material [Billie Holiday] had performed prior to integrating 'Strange Fruit' into her repertoire, she reaffirmed among her musical colleagues the import of employing their medium in the quest for social justice, thus perpetuating its musical voice."[3]

Billie Holiday, using the instruments of her body, was tuning us into the frequencies of timeless ancestral truths that aggravate and settle the soul. She was singing the blues while challenging us to do better. She was in service as she was serving. Audre Lorde noted that Black women "are expected to use our anger only in the service of other people's salvation or learning. But that time is over."[4] Indeed, the anger and pain experienced by Black—and Brown—women and girls must also serve their own liberation.

More than a conduit for marginalized voices, the blues is a means to stimulate radical possibilities.

⌒

The blues emerged in the nineteenth century as an African American musical genre rooted in the phrasing of Negro spirituals, the work songs of enslaved, impoverished people and the cultural shouts and hollers that traditionally express sorrow, betrayal, and harm. But the blues was also an underground musical railroad to survival. While typically associated with the articulation of pain and revenge, the blues is also about *becoming*. In some cases, the expression is about a longing for freedom. Though associated with men, the blues has also been a destination for women seeking to articulate their truths, particularly as an expression of the racialized gender bias shaping their lives. Billie Holiday, Bessie Smith, Gertrude "Ma" Rainey, Big Mama Thornton, Koko Taylor, and others who would later weave their blueprints into rock and roll, rhythm and blues, country, and funk understood that their freedom could be accessed through their wails, moans, and dances. Millions of people consume the blues as entertainment without acknowledging its most important contributions to the freedom struggle: a platform for truth telling, a form of resistance, and thus a pathway to healing and learning.

Wise women have known this for centuries—it's why the hum of a grandmother or rocking embrace of an aunt feels so good. Embedded in these motions is the magic that should guide us in creating schools that are responsive to the conditions and experiences of Black girls and other girls of color. The blues is about bearing witness to contradictions and then working through them to bring about critical, intellectually responsible thinking and action. When blues women tap their hips, sway their bodies, or growl their pleas for justice into the melody of a song, they are creating an emergent healing condition.

This element of the blues, while undertheorized, is instructive, particularly when working with girls and young women who have shared some of the same experiences as these blues women. Amid the drinking and exploration of other vices, blues women also center love in their unapologetic display of vulnerability and their expressive resistance to being "played" by those in positions of power. When "something's got a hold" on them, they get creative in order to survive. Their feisty brand of feminism (or womanism) breathes life onto a dead-end street. Here lies a tremendous opportunity for a pedagogy of liberation, an educational approach infused with principles of healing. Why healing? Because that is what will enable schools to truly become locations for learning.

But which school-based strategies foster educational justice for our most vulnerable students? This is the question I explore in this book. I suggest that the blues, as an expression of Black pain and power, can help educators, parents, students, and community members reimagine schools as places that counter the criminalization of Black and Brown girls.

This is not a book about educational or justice *reform*. This is about restructuring our entire approach to the education of Black and Brown girls in crisis. Schools, though conceived as institutions to prepare future generations for participation in society, instead often exacerbate conditions that undermine full citizenship—along with students' personal sense of humanity. School-to-confinement pathways—the policies, practices, conditions, and prevailing consciousness that render children and adolescents vulnerable to contact with the juvenile court and criminal legal system—are structures of violence we should critique and dismantle.

In school districts throughout the country, disproportionately high levels of Black, Latina, and Indigenous girls are struggling to realize their true identities as scholars. Too often they are pushed out of schools and into participation in underground economies, in which they're vulnerable to exploitation, violence, and other harms. For these girls, defiance, as an expression of dissent, is criminalized; it is treated as an offense, rather than understood as a form of critical thinking.

In *Pushout: The Criminalization of Black Girls in Schools*, I explored how this specifically manifests in the educational experiences of Black girls and, through data and the stories of marginalized girls, how we might become more aware of a phenomenon that was previously obscured and undertheorized. In the years since that book's publication, I have had the opportunity to visit several schools and programs throughout the country working to improve outcomes for Black girls and other girls of color. In my discussions, I reviewed the key elements associated with the criminalization of Black girls in schools and guided educators, students, and the broader community of concerned adults in how to use the book as more than a one-read experience. These visits were often conducted in tandem with community and/or parent meetings, providing an opportunity to lay out the facts and recurring dynamics—to groups of girls and young women, teachers, principals, parents, and district leaders—that illuminate how school pushout and student criminalization harm Black girls and other girls of color.

Black girls remain the only group of girls to experience negative outcomes at every point along the full discipline continuum, from suspension, corporal punishment, and expulsion to arrest and referral to law enforcement, but growing rates among other girls of color also give us cause for alarm. Latinas, some of them also identifying as Indigenous and/or Black, are increasingly experiencing exclusionary discipline and other negative educational outcomes.* These trends suggest that building safe learning spaces

---

* The U.S. Census collects and reports data for "Hispanic" populations as an ethnicity, rather than as a racial group. As such, people of Latinx/Hispanic descent may also be included among populations characterized as Black, White, Asian, Indigenous, or Other. This may obscure trends among Latinx populations who are of mixed racial heritage. According to analyses conducted by the National Black Women's Justice Institute, Latinx girls in middle school are particularly vulnerable to exclusionary discipline. Nationwide, Latinx girls in middle schools are twice as likely as their white counterparts to experience one or more out-of-school suspensions and they are almost twice as likely to be referred to law enforcement and arrested on campus. (M. Inniss-Thompson, *Summary of Discipline Data for Girls in U.S. Public Schools*, National Black Women's Justice Institute, 2018.)

requires developing racially and ethnically specific approaches to healing, in addition to the universal changes in our thinking that will enable us to address the differential treatment and outcomes for girls of color.

Each visit to a school or community brings new opportunities for interacting with girls of color who grapple daily with the harm stemming from school discipline, criminalization, and academic underachievement. On this journey, I regularly observe schools and classrooms that are engaged in positive, innovative, and promising approaches to educating and supporting girls of color. These gems were too good to keep to myself, so, in the tradition of blues women, travel with me on the road to explore stories and strategies that will increase our collective capacity to produce schools that do freedom work.

Instead of analyzing the policies and practices that *undermine* good outcomes, I invite you into the world that schools, in partnership with gender-responsive, culture-specific programs, are building to interrupt school-to-confinement pathways. I offer examples where Black and Brown girls are encouraged to sing a rhythm and dance a blues *toward their own liberation*, where caring adults alongside them create conditions for healing. Together we will witness how healing permits these girls and young women to feel empowered and to learn.

In this book, I center several open inquiries: What does it mean, in real time, to uplift a healing form of justice in service of education? How do we create and operate safe, thriving learning spaces that neither problematize girls of color nor respond to their mistakes with lasting or irreparable harm? What does it mean to adopt a pedagogical practice that rejects the notion that loud or "sassy" girls are disorderly, defiant, and disposable? How can we instill in girls the tools they need to combat oppression, rather than reinforce or succumb to it? And what do schools look like when they reject the tools of oppression and criminalization?

Children and adolescents who are most vulnerable to school pushout are resilient, but *relationships* sustain their well-being. Places where adults believe in the promise of all children are essential for healthy relationships to flourish. This is the power of transforming schools from conduits to prison into incubators of excellence. Embarking on such a project requires tools to challenge and reverse the growing pathologizing of our nation's learning spaces—and the people inside them.

The assertion that nothing can be done to counter the criminalization of girls of color is false. Once you know this, you can't pretend you don't. As parents, educators, and concerned adults, our intentions and actions are either part of the problem or part of the solution. Interrupting school-to-confinement pathways for girls of color demands that we engage students in the co-construction of their learning. The pedagogy I propose in the following pages is a blues. It is a blues that is built on narrative and rests on data. It is a blues for Black and Brown girls who have had enough and deserve better from all of us. It is the work and the song of the teacher, as a partner in education. It is political. It is practical. It is love, and it is power.

Interlude

"You Have to Be Compassionate"

We're dealing with children, so although we want to politicize education and make it into a corporate entity, they're *children*. They're people. They're individual souls that in some cases have been on the planet for only four or five years. They're really in their formative years. They're still learning language. They're still learning what is socially appropriate in different environments. You have to gather everyone together and assess individually where each student is.

Kids have been socialized in different ways, so they're going to come into the classroom in a lot of different ways. If you find that a student is hungry, you have to find a way to help them with those basic needs and still educate them.

You have to ask, what are my obstacles? How can I overcome those obstacles and still meet the student's educational goals? It has to be very intentional. You have to be compassionate, because you have to manage *everyone*. The kids are the priority—and then there's everyone else. When the kids leave your space, they should be better in some way. They should be better than how they came to you. If you're not on the page to make the kids better, then you don't belong here. Yes, everybody needs a paycheck, but there are other ways to get a paycheck. If you are not interested in making these kids better, then you don't belong here.

Every year, you're building on something. Maybe last year, a kid cried every time she had to write her name. Maybe in the next grade, it might take her twenty-five minutes to write her name, but she's not crying anymore, because she's learned a coping mechanism. We have to be very clear on what it is that we want from the kids. We can't be lackadaisical with the children of color in our classrooms. We have to dig deep. People were getting whipped for learning how to read. People got their hands chopped off for learning how to read. And you're going to come in here and not care that this little Black kid in your class can't read words better than when she came into your classroom? No. We have to take this job seriously.

All teachers have to be about their business. They have to be intentional about how they are teaching this child. With little girls, like the kindergarteners, it's the mouth. The talking back. They may tantrum, kick the floor, or refuse to do the work or come out of a space. In my school, they don't expel. We know our principal loves the kids, and we love the kids too.

I had a young lady in my class who was okay when we started off. Then progressively she was getting a little busier, to the point where she was getting out of her seat. I was like, you know what? I'm not going to really make a big deal out of certain behaviors. Only if she makes a physical threat to the other children will I say something. When she started throwing pencils at the other kids, taking the desk and pushing it into other kids, then I had to be like, "Okay, we're done."

In her case, it was all home. Her mom's personality was very combative. The way the mother communicates was very rough. Unfortunately, she had done some time in prison. The girl's dad, as I understood it, was cheating on her mother, so her parents broke up, and with that breach, there was a lot of pain and grief. The father was shot. It was bad. From what I understood, the police were often called to the house to break up some dispute. If that's what you learn, if nobody is giving you another "language" to use, then you think everybody communicates that way. So, when you don't get your way, you're going to tantrum.

To deal with the issue, I kept in contact with the person who came to pick her up, but I didn't call the mother every day, because if she *could* have done something different, she would have by then. This behavior had been going on since pre-K.

I told the girl, "I'm not going to call your mother every day because, number one, I don't have the time. Number two, when you come here, we have too many things to do. But I'm going to tell you what, both of us are responsible for your education." I was very clear and consistent about that.

Thankfully, as rough a reputation as her mother had, she was never disrespectful to me. When I called her, I tried not to be accusatory. I said, "I just want you to know that I have to keep in communication with you because she's *our* child. She's my daughter, too, for the school year. I want you to be clear that I will always be honest with you about what I say to her and what I do."

When the kids say, "I'm going to tell my mother," I say, "Please do, so we can sit down and talk about this. I'm not scared to talk to your momma. I'm not scared!"

Anyway, this girl's mother was always very open and never disrespectful. Her mother felt that she needed to be tested and might need a smaller setting. So they tested her and found that the problem wasn't her learning ability, but her behavior. She was put into a class with more adults in the room who could help work with her.

You have to be compassionate. Teaching is a calling.

Suzanne
Kindergarten teacher
New York

Track 1
Fit to Wear a Crown

The Case for Suspending Exclusionary Discipline

You told me that I was like an angel,
Told me I was fit to wear a crown.

. . .

You put me on a pedestal,
And then you let me down.

> —*Al Dubin and Harry Warren, "You Let Me*
> *Down," as sung by Billie Holiday*
> *(Brunswick Records, 1935)*

I met Stephanie Patton, the principal of a public middle school for girls in Columbus, Ohio, in 2016.[1] At a community meeting, she announced that after a lot of deep reflection and discussion about the criminalization of Black girls, she and her faculty would no longer punish their students for having a "bad attitude." She had noticed that responding to her mostly African American student body with exclusionary discipline was only contributing to the harm these girls were experiencing. Instead, she developed a school discipline continuum that included mentoring, positive behavioral interventions and supports,* restorative conferencing, and an advisory program that starts girls off each day by promoting their self-worth, communication skills, and goal-setting. Only if *absolutely necessary*—after everything else had been explored and exhausted—were suspensions used as a last-resort intervention. Ms. Patton and her team were committed to doing everything they could to avoid punishing girls in a way that would make future contact with the juvenile court or criminal legal system more likely. They began by building an infrastructure to support this decision.

Along the corridors of the school are strategically placed whiteboards with quotes shared by faculty, staff, and students, such as "I never dreamed about success; I worked for it" or "Your life is your story; write well, edit often." In small areas of the school, there are pillows and comfortable seats for girls who need a moment to collect their thoughts, take a breath, or regroup after (or before) a conflict occurs. There are three additional classrooms that are used as "time out" spaces for girls who need a course correction. One is a PBIS room filled with material incentives (puzzles, materials for arts and crafts, decorative pillows, etc.) for students, and the other two are dedicated to in-school suspension (ISS) activities.

---

* The phrase *positive behavioral interventions and supports* (PBIS) refers to a multi-tier set of guidelines and practices for schools to improve academic, social, and emotional outcomes for students. The system was developed by the Technical Assistance Center of the Office of Special Education Programs of the U.S. Department of Education.

In many educational spaces, ISS still results in a loss of instruction time—students do little, if any, academic work. However, at Ms. Patton's school, the ISS classrooms are structured to respond to the academic and social-emotional needs of the girls who find themselves there. In one classroom, the "student center," students have use of computers and spend their time completing academic tasks or other socially relevant, educational tasks, and they must show that they have completed the work before returning to the classroom. The room is set up classroom-lecture style, with desks that seat two to a table. On the wall is a giant butterfly, prominently displayed next to an excerpt from Maya Angelou's poem, "Still I Rise."

"I see all of the completed assignments," Ms. Patton said. "There is accountability because they know the principal will be reviewing their work."

Girls in the school are encouraged to engage in advocacy and activism as part of their healing process. When I asked Ms. Patton what that meant, she gave an example of a group of girls who used their ISS assignment to research resource disparities among district public schools and craft a letter to educational policy makers demanding change. "Even though there are proper channels for that sort of complaint," she said with a smile, "those are my girls."

The other alternative classroom is a space that girls use for quiet, more reflective activities. The room is filled with couches, pillows, rugs, a large bulletin board with pictures of students making projects, and magenta drapes that cast a pink hue from wall to wall. The open space facilitates a flow of energy, and to the right is a Maker's Corner for girls who are drawn to tactile activities as a way to calm down.

Ms. Patton says that she hardly uses the space for punitive intervention. "Most of our students come here to proactively work on projects with a teacher, not as a form of punishment," she said.

By setting the intention of her school to respond to the underlying issues associated with student misbehavior, Ms. Patton has led her school in efforts that are significantly shifting the trajectories of students. That academic year, attendance was higher and suspensions decreased. She had not expelled anyone that year, and she noticed an increase in students' commitment to collective accountability when there was a problem on campus, particularly bullying.

"Our motto is 'Real queens fix each other's crowns,'" she said to me with a wink.

⌢

To fall from favor is emotionally taxing and physically draining, but when someone believes herself to be "fit to wear a crown," she embraces her full potential. One of the girls I spoke with at Ms. Patton's school referred to being Black as being part of "royalty." To her, racial pride was at the center of her belief in herself as a member of this learning community. She was worthy of investment, worthy of praise. While most children may not be of actual royal lineage, when they believe they're "fit to wear a crown," they're likely to feel worthy of redemption. Even when they make a mistake, they understand that the response is not intended to derail their learning or their lives, but rather to reconnect them to their true purpose. The neglect—or erasure—of this identity can lead to girls internalizing harmful historical narratives about their inferiority, and could even leave them feeling as if no one cares about them at all.

For teachers and other educators, reinforcing the royal mindset requires a commitment not to equate accountability with discipline and punishment. We have conflated them for too long. Rejecting this false equation should be the norm, a baseline for all learning institutions. It isn't something to consider, debate, or negotiate. As a premise, it is simply too faulty and dangerous.

Overall, students in U.S. schools are effective learners who do not exhibit behavior that warrants exclusionary discipline. However, racial disparities continue to plague those girls who do get into trouble in school.[2] The research on Black girls and other girls of color in assessments of school discipline shows that the actions that lead to their suspension or expulsion do include fighting but are more often minor infractions whose punishment is not in fact about protecting the school from violence. Girls of color are more likely than others to be suspended for violations of school rules (e.g., dress codes embedded in codes of conduct), for failure to comply with adult requests (e.g., producing identification when requested), and for subjective, even arbitrary, infractions that leave ample room for personal biases to reign supreme, such as "willful defiance."[3]

In Kentucky, where researchers Edward Morris and Brea Perry examined the specific infractions leading to the use of exclusionary discipline statewide, they found that African American girls were more likely than white girls to be suspended for subjectively determined "violations" of school order, and that the racial disparities were more prevalent among girls than boys. The study acknowledges that "black girls are much more likely than other girls to be cited for infractions such as dress code violations, disobedience, disruptive behavior, and aggressive behavior— and these gaps are far wider than the gaps between black boys and boys of other races for these offenses."[4] Many of the specific infractions, including dress code violations, disruptive behavior, and cell phone use, involved discretionary judgments that are often made through a racialized and gendered lens. Morris and Perry found that Black boys were twice as likely as boys of European descent to receive a disciplinary referral; however, Black girls were three times as likely as girls of European descent to receive a referral, based largely on the school administrators' interpretation of behavior as disruptive or disobedient.[5]

The culture of punishment that has dominated education for more than two decades is now being critically examined by many institutions and advocates, particularly as part of the current revulsion against stubborn racism, sexism, homophobia, transphobia, and lingering xenophobia. Unfortunately, as the nation struggles to confront the vestiges of white supremacist ideology and its impact on education, some of our schools continue to respond to crises with fear rather than love.

By and large, schools are operating under the assumption that only intimidation changes behavior. This is nothing new. Just as "youthful misbehavior" has been dated to the beginning of recorded history, evidence of student violence in American schools has dated back more than a century. Religion and moral instruction were at the center of education in the American colonial era, planting seeds for a discipline philosophy rooted in the belief that children were predisposed to sin. The prevailing belief was that the most effective strategy to curb these sinful behaviors was to give kids an ultimatum: either practice extreme dedication to obedience or suffer extraordinary physical consequences.[6] The Bible-inspired maxim "Spare the rod, spoil the child" was the order of the day. Evidence of the lengths to which this idea was taken is found in the words of Puritan leader John Cotton, who proposed to the Massachusetts General Court in 1641 that "rebellious children, whether they continue in riot or drunkenesse, after due correction from their parents, or whether they curse or smite their parents, be put to death."[7]

While extreme, this response to youthful misbehavior reflects the deeply entrenched nature of violent course correction in our public consciousness, particularly as it applies to those who occupy the status of minors. Cotton's open request is a prime example of just how irrational some of our public responses to the behavior of young people have been historically. Death? Really? As egregious as this example may seem, common approaches to student misbehavior today are similarly misaligned with moral, evidence-based methods.

Many school disciplinary measures reflect a belief that children should be forced into acceptable school behavior by intimidation, suppression, isolation, or arrest. In at least twenty-three states and jurisdictions, there are "disturbing schools" laws that make it an actual crime to be "obnoxious" or, as in South Carolina, to "interfere with or to disturb in any way or in any place the students or teachers of any school or college."[8] We have developed a robust infrastructure that responds to the negative behaviors of students with harsh punishment, often exclusion or force, ostensibly to mitigate conflict in schools. The assumption is that by removing students who exhibit problematic behavior *from* schools, we can produce safety *in* schools.

Amid pervasive racism, every form of exclusionary discipline—suspension, expulsion, corporal punishment, referral to law enforcement, and arrest on campus—reinforces stereotypes and fear of Black and Brown girls, who are disproportionately pushed out of school. Our fear has spiraled out of control, and very young girls are being suspended, even expelled for throwing tantrums or taking candy from a teacher's desk.[9]

We can do better.

Believing in the Promise of All Children

Suspensions have become so common that people often reject the idea that they are inherently harmful.

I was a guest on a Northern California radio program when a father called in to say that he wanted all of the "bad girls" out of the school so that his daughter could learn. He said it with conviction—and I accepted his challenge. It wasn't the first time I'd heard from fearful parents or a concerned public servant about what could happen if we keep every girl labeled as "disruptive" in school. Many people have an anecdote about a girl who was suspended from a school and instantly the conditions improved for other children. In response, I always pose the question, Did the conditions *actually* improve?

If a student is causing harm and triggering pain among other students, there must be an intervention. She may need another classroom or a different educational team, but if we think that everything would be "fine" just because a "bad" or "disruptive" girl is no longer attending classes with other students, we're mistaken. Just as removing a cancerous cell from a human body can temporarily send someone into remission—temporarily saving a life—unless the conditions change in the system, the cancer is likely to form again. Schools that report having minimal or no suspensions or expulsions understand that the intentions and culture of a school have a lot to do with how students behave and what happens when they behave in ways that disrupt learning. Radically shifting the outcomes for girls of color, and for their classmates who experience conflict with them, isn't possible unless the goal to do precisely that is shaping a school's intentions and culture.

Albert Einstein once said that "the worst thing seems to be for a school principally to work with methods of fear, force, and artificial authority. Such treatment destroys the sound sentiments, the sincerity, and the self-confidence of the pupil."[10] Exclusionary discipline is significantly associated with a failure to complete school and with poor student achievement.[11] Even one suspension is associated with an increased probability of future contact with the criminal legal system.[12] Girls with an education are less likely to be poor, to be involved in violent relationships, and to be arrested. Lawrence DeRidder wrote in 1990 that experiencing suspension and expulsion "hurries the dropout process" and lowers academic performance, making kids vulnerable to school pushout, participation in underground economies, and trouble with the law.[13] In the words of professors Russ Skiba and Reece Peterson, "Indiscriminate use of force without regard for its effects is the hallmark of authoritarianism, incompatible with the functioning of a democracy, and certainly incompatible with the transmission of democratic values to children."[14]

Fixing each other's crowns requires that we explore precisely what is disrupting the positioning or composition of the crown. Our challenge is not to mediate student misbehavior, but rather to better understand that this misbehavior—when it is a real disruption and not a construct of policies designed to criminalize normal adolescent and childhood development—is almost always associated with a student's perception of, and reaction to, harm.

The Brain and Student "Misbehavior"

Misbehavior is often interpreted as a violation of rules, laws, or agreements. When girls of color "misbehave" in schools, they are typically treated as if something is wrong with them, often without considering the conditions that sparked the action in question. Recently I traveled to upstate New York, to Rochester, to visit with a group of Black and Latina girls enrolled in one of the city's magnet high schools. During this meeting, we discussed conditions in schools that either respond to or facilitate conflict among the girls of color. When I asked how schools typically respond when there's a conflict, girls most often mentioned suspension. As an alternative, some schools offered opportunities to "reconcile" issues through conversation, but the girls noted that it was usually *an adult talking to them*, rather than giving them a chance to express what happened or *facilitating a conversation* between the conflicting parties. In many schools, girls of color are not offered alternatives to suspension—even when a school has alternatives in its toolkit—because administrators perceive them as unwilling to participate in restorative circles or other processes intended to mitigate or avoid exclusionary discipline.

However, in discussions with girls who have been excluded from this type of programming, I found that it is not their *unwillingness* to participate, but their *capacity* to do so in that moment.

"When I'm upset, I can't form words," one student explained. "My head is spinning. . . . I need time to calm down before mediation."

If our intention is to facilitate healing, we need to meet our girls where they are, rather than expect them to be where we want them to be.

Girls of color who fight or exhibit other problematic behaviors in schools are not inherently bad or sinful, nor are they necessarily premeditating defiance or acts of aggression. These girls are eager for the adults in their lives to respond to them with attention to the initial conflict, the root of their discontent, not their reaction to it. Failing to fully consider or attempt to discover why these girls are in conflict prevents concerned adults from contributing positively to a resolution. In practice, this failure might look like "keeping the peace," but it's actually throwing a blanket over the core issues.

The growing body of neuroscientific research exploring how the brain perceives threat and how this affects student behavior in schools is a critical anchor for discussions of student misbehavior. In her book *Culturally Responsive Teaching and the Brain*, Zaretta Hammond writes:

> Relationships exist at the intersection of mind-body. They are the precursor to learning. When anyone experiences others in an environment like a classroom that is inattentive or hostile, the body picks

up that information through the autonomic nervous system and sends it up to the [reticular activating system*] and amygdala. There the amygdala gets the information that it's not socially, emotionally, or intellectually safe and sends out a distress signal to the body. The body starts to produce stress hormones that make learning nearly impossible. Even if the environment isn't hostile but simply unwelcoming, the brain doesn't produce enough oxytocin and begins to experience anxiety. This anxiety triggers the sympathetic nervous system, making one think he is in danger because the brain doesn't experience a sense of community.[15]

Brain functions regulated by the amygdala shape our "fight, flight, or freeze" instincts, protecting us from harm in moments of crisis. The stress hormone cortisol automatically is released in the brain when a person feels threatened, interrupting her capacity to problem-solve or learn. In many conversations with Black and Brown girls who have experienced exclusionary discipline, they admit that they "don't know what happened" or that they "just snapped" before engaging in a school fight. Similarly, conversations with teachers reveal their recognition that girls "go into a zone" and that once they're there, the aggression may escalate, at which point it's difficult to pull them out of it. These scenarios are extraordinarily stressful for everyone when they occur.

---

* The reticular activating system (RAS) is the networking function of the brain that controls conscious awareness, focus, and alertness, as well as sleep.

There is an African proverb that says, "Until the lions have their own historian, the story of the hunt will glorify the hunter." But we know that "the hunt" affects much more than just the hunter and the lion. It affects the fly on the lion's tail, the zebra and antelope that may be watching—and it affects the very land upon which the hunt is taking place. Everyone is affected by the hunt. Constructing safety is a group project.

Occasional stress is a normal part of human life. However, to experience stress continuously, as do many of the high-risk girls who witness or participate in school-based violence, impairs a young person's ability to cope with adversity. Chronic stress impairs the capacity of students (and teachers) to build positive relationships, and to process information that is being communicated in the learning environment. According to the Harvard University Center on the Developing Child, toxic stress may manifest among children when they experience "strong, frequent, and/or prolonged adversity—such as physical or emotional abuse, chronic neglect, caregiver substance abuse or mental illness, exposure to violence, and/or the accumulated burdens of family economic hardship—without adequate adult support."[16] These and other adverse childhood experiences (ACEs) interrupt the developmental trajectory by interfering with memory and learning, attention and focus, and the regulation of emotions. ACEs can and often do hamper people well into adulthood.[17]

Memory, focus, and regulation of emotion are all critical functions needed to operate successfully in a classroom. The foundation for generating alternatives to exclusionary discipline is to create learning spaces that are free from the kinds of conditions that produce or exacerbate chronic stress. Safe spaces are essential for alternatives to be effective and flourish. Safety is not a condition that can be implemented, however. It must be co-constructed through a set of agreements with all of those involved in the creation of a learning space. In schools, students must collaborate with adults in deciding what constitutes "safety" on campus.

Preparing to transform schools and other learning spaces is as important as the work of actually transforming them. Educators who have not done the necessary work of rigorously examining their own biases are typically not prepared to lead this co-constructive work. In order to partner with young people, an adult must recognize both her biases and her areas of expertise. It's also crucial for adults to maintain openness and genuinely value children as viable partners in efforts to create safety. Considering the lessons our girls learn when they are pushed away from the classroom will help the process honor and account for invisible factors. Real safety emerges from strong relationships among school personnel, parents, and students, including key individuals outside of the class or school. A focus on the voids— on those who are not in the room—can actually *increase* our own capacity to deliver educational justice. What is happening with the children and adolescents who are *not* in the room is critical to the development of strategies to engage those students differently. Oppression, and its physical and emotional impacts, thrives in conditions of isolation. When girls get in trouble, we should consider ways to bring them in closer, rather than pushing them away.

As Audre Lorde once reminded us, "The master's tools will never dismantle the master's house. They may allow us temporarily to beat him at his own game, but they will never enable us to bring about genuine change."[18] Similarly, exclusionary discipline might give a school a momentary reprieve from conflict, but it does nothing to dismantle the structures that produced the conflict in the first place. It deepens the original harm that led to conflict, and fails to facilitate spaces for healing.

Education is freedom work. In order for freedom to infuse and dominate the popular culture of our institutions, and the communities being educated in them, education cannot be understood as an exercise of privilege—or punishment. To focus on the absence of children is to acknowledge that there is an opportunity to improve our institutions so that all children can be there. In a culture that prioritizes the "exclusive," uplifting a paradigm of *inclusion* is arduous work—and an intentional rejection of the politics of fear that perpetuate violence in and out of the classroom.

Spare the Rod . . .

A *New York Times* article examining abuses at a Louisiana charter school noted, "Pupils [were] humiliated in front of their peers and racial groups [were] pitted against one another. . . . More than a half dozen students said they had witnessed [the principal] choking their schoolmates, and three students observed him slam others on desks. Another three students said they saw [the principal] place a child with autism in a closet."[19]

Corporal punishment in schools is one of the world's most egregious and dangerous forms of school discipline. By now, to find proponents of it, we should have to blow the dust from archival materials about seventeenth-century teachers who beat their students until they bled.[20] Unfortunately, a version of this practice is still expressly legal—in the twenty-first century—in fifteen states, with another seven states taking a more neutral position of not *prohibiting* it but not banning it altogether.[21]

Between the late 1970s and 1994, there was a "steady decline" in public school use of corporal punishment, largely attributed to a ban in twenty-five states.[22] As of 1994, however, 86 percent of Southerners still expressed a favorable attitude toward corporal punishment in schools.[23] A more recent assessment found that "the states that continue to allow corporal punishment have a greater percentage of children in the general population, higher rates of child poverty and child mortality, lower college graduation rates, and lower per-pupil education expenditures than states that have banned school corporal punishment."[24]

Corporal punishment is recognized as a violation of human rights according to the United Nations Convention on the Rights of the Child, but the United States has yet to ratify this agreement. The convention explicitly calls for each nation to implement processes to uphold "legislative, administrative, social and educational measures to protect the child from all forms of physical or mental violence, injury or abuse, neglect or negligent treatment," among other abuses and tortures.[25]

Notwithstanding this global standard, African American girls are more than three times more likely than white girls to experience physical punishment. While only 16 percent of girls enrolled in public schools, Black girls are 46 percent of girls who experience corporal punishment and nearly 32 percent of girls being restrained in public schools.[26]

The use of corporal punishment was widespread among European cultures for centuries, and its use in racist North American society further dehumanized people as a rationalization for white supremacy.[27] Teaching enslaved or impoverished Black and colonized Brown children that misbehavior would be met with beatings, burnings, lynchings, and other forms of torture was effective in instilling fear as motivation to "act right." Whippings were basic to problem solving. For the children, physical and emotional torture was synonymous with "learning" in Western-oriented spaces. Violence was an effective behavioral modification tool; schools would operate as if children needed to experience pain in order to learn a lesson. However, violence was also a powerful facilitator of the racialized gender oppression that sustains the social and cultural inequities that produce educational disparities and poor outcomes for girls of color.[28]

Using force may modify how someone *acts*, but there are consequences to being forced to act contrary to one's feelings. It impacts a person's psychological and emotional development. The use of corporal punishment in schools has been associated with poor problem solving and a host of other negative outcomes, including:

- *Increased aggression and oppositional response to conflict.* Social cognitive theory proposes that children who observe and experience violence may be conditioned to reproduce and/or mimic it. If children are shown aggression as a model for problem solving, they are likely to engage in it as a response to conflict. Kids who are hit learn that hitting solves problems. Researchers have found that not only is corporal punishment associated with increased aggression, but it is also associated with higher rates of sadness and anxiety,[29] and of fear, which may lead to more forceful responses to adults who cause physical harm.[30]

- *Increased substance dependency or abuse and negative mental health outcomes.* Experiencing corporal punishment as a child is associated with adult depression and increased probability of suicide, as well as alcoholism and gender-based violence.[31]

- *Poor brain development and deregulation of behavior.* Chronic exposure to harsh corporal punishment has been associated with a reduction in the brain's prefrontal cortical gray matter volume (GMV), which neurologists have found to play a "crucial role in social cognition as well as functional organization."[32] GMV is also associated with self-awareness, so exposure to harsh corporal punishment has been found to *reduce* a child's ability to monitor her or his own actions, thereby increasing the risk of exposure to more violence.[33]

There are no redeeming qualities to the use of violence to "teach" children and adolescents how to behave—in school or at home. This practice should be buried with other antiquated, biased, and oppressive ideas about maintaining social order.

Foundations for Transformation

Transforming the learning landscape for girls of color necessitates that schools consistently reject actions, philosophies, pedagogies, and principles that we know to be harmful and disruptive to their development. If our goal is to ensure that educational institutions are not woven into the tapestry of harm for marginalized girls, we have to find a fabric that disrupts the existing pattern. Changing our approach to negative student behavior begins with setting the *intention* to do so. Setting our intentions with clarity and commitment opens up new possibilities and provides a foundation for change.

The foundations of punitive school discipline, currently practiced by so many of our nation's schools, are violent and oppressive. Centuries of responding to negative student behavior with fear produced a discipline paradigm that exacerbates harm. On one hand, punitive and authoritarian responses have led to behavior modifications that privilege the priorities of law and order. On the other hand, these models collectively reinforce the notion that youthful dissent is a "crime," and that a violent response to that dissent is an effective remedy. But emergent and established research speak a different truth.

Paulo Freire invited us to understand that the pedagogy of oppression is "an instrument for their critical discovery that both [the oppressed] and their oppressors are manifestations of dehumanization. . . . Liberation is thus a childbirth, and a painful one."[34] What we model for girls and young women of color plants seeds. Those seeds will bear fruit that feeds a nation: the systems we build, the opportunities we create, and the strategies we use to build knowledge. "The solution is not to 'integrate' [oppressed communities] into the structure of oppression, but to transform that structure so that they can become 'beings for themselves,'" suggests Freire.[35]

Anti-oppressive classroom management strategies for girls of color—those that intend to facilitate a real freedom and safety so learning can take place—first and foremost reflect agreements established between students and adults. If policies or the prevailing consciousness in a classroom or school embraces racist, sexist, ableist, homophobic, transphobic, and xenophobic ideas, then the learning environment is not safe. A feeling of danger engenders conflict; rarely does it mitigate or prevent it. When we ask why girls of color, especially Black girls, are overrepresented along the school discipline continuum, we need to understand the conditions they perceive as threatening to their well-being, then understand that their behavior is a response to those conditions.

Disruptive behaviors are actions that prevent learning from taking place. Good pedagogy that takes the whole person into account understands clearly that disruptive Black and Brown girls have faced disruption in their lives. Education can repair the damage. The question is not *who she is* but rather what has happened in her life. We have to stop asking, "What's wrong with her?" or "How fast can we get her out of this school?" and instead ask, "What's happened to her?" A deeper understanding of her conditions may prevent her from being labeled a problem.

Other questions might include:

- What specifically has happened to provoke this behavior? To what is the student responding? When did it begin?
- What supports do I need in the classroom to restore relationships of safety and trust in school? Who can help me access or develop those supports?

- What internal work do I and other adults need to do to recognize the humanity of students who may need additional intervention? ✳
- How can I work with my students, their parents, and school leadership to change the conditions in my classroom so that girls of color can learn effectively?

Schools that reduce their emphasis on exclusionary discipline are not operating "free-for-alls" where disorder and chaos are rampant. Instead, these are schools that have facilitated a climate in which collective responsibility, accountability, and trust form a new normal that is expected not only from students, but also from the administrators, the teachers, and others who are involved in the school's daily activities. Our goal is to fix each other's crowns, not to throw out those girls struggling to keep their crowns intact.

That is true accountability.

Interlude

"They Are Survivors"

How do you measure the level of adversity that girls face?

You can say "adversity," "at-risk," "vulnerability," but to a policy maker who is talking dollars and cents, they really don't mean anything.

We discovered ACEs during a federal roundtable on trauma and realized that the system's simplicity was part of the magic. It was actually quite unbelievable that ten items could help to inform not only the service practice, but the advocacy work—and that it could be a key to unlock some self-discovery for the young women and girls themselves. So, that's why we use it across all of our agencies. The way that it serves to *self-empower* the young women was perhaps more a surprise . . . we didn't expect it to have the tremendous impact that it has had on young women.

We use the ACEs survey with the young women who are leading programs, developing programs, and the young women who are doing local and national advocacy. We don't require them to take it, but we present the information as a tool. Almost 100 percent of them *want* to take it, because it explains, using science and facts, the context and realities of their lives. Now, they've faced much more adversity than the ten items on the ACEs survey, but because there's data behind it, it's a pretty powerful tool.

Initially, many people were critical of our use of the ACEs tool with these young women and girls, believing that they would be triggered. But in fact, they're not. It really unlocks this understanding that they are *survivors*. Their strength and courage and tenacity against these odds is what makes them survivors. A lot of them cry when they hear it—not because it's triggering, but because it's liberating.

The other thing it does, which we don't talk about as much, is create an opportunity to address the shame. Whether its sexual abuse, physical abuse, emotional abuse, neglect, parents incarcerated—there's a lot of shame with that. Our agencies that run schools use the tool. Initially they were resistant, but they've come full circle. Whether you directly address it or not, it's there and affecting everything they do. They use it in schools and as parent training of sorts, as a way to understand that these are not decisions that you are making only for yourselves, but also for your children, and here's the science to prove it.

What the ACEs tool does is say, it's not really about the shame, it's the context. It's about conditions that you had no control of—and *that* begins to chip away at the shame that says they should be doing better in their lives, that they should have done better in schools—the "coulda, shoulda, woulda" type of thing. They don't really feel that anymore, and they're able to translate it to their siblings and their parents' understandings. It gives them a way to talk to their family about how they, as a family and across generations, ended up where they are. For a lot of them, who felt that they couldn't succeed in school, because they thought they weren't "smart enough" or because they had all of these issues, it allows them to transform their image of what they can do and who they can be.

Jeannette Pai-Espinosa
National Crittenton
Oregon

God Bless the Child That's Got Her Own

Responding to Trauma

Yes, the strong gets more
While the weak ones fade.
Empty pockets don't ever make the grade.
—*Arthur Herzog and Billie Holiday, "God Bless the*
Child" (Okeh Records, 1942).

"**I** want to know how you get your Bantu knots to stay in," a girl from Iowa City asked me, slouching in her chair and twirling her fingers around her own braids.

Without hesitation, I explained how I styled my locs into the knots.

"Hair tutorial!" a couple of girls shouted. "Ayyye!"

I'd been asked to share a few words with the girls about my journey in this work when the girls launched into a barrage of questions about my personal styling that day. This is not uncommon—many girls are interested in how adult women achieve a style they think is appealing. After building trust by working through the surface-level styling questions, a girl asked what has been my greatest challenge in life and how I overcame it.

The question was deeply personal, but those of us who inter-act with youth regularly know they are often not shy about ask-ing personal questions. They seek to know the *real* us. It's how they remove our masks for us and remind us of the connections that are necessary to build relationships that matter. Part of my answer to them included a reveal of my own personal and family history of trauma and the ways in which it informs my approach to advocating for justice.

As I spoke, I could see recognition in their faces. They finally saw me—not just my Bantu knots. And I saw them.

God bless the child.

⌒

Trauma.

A blow to the head. The sudden removal of a parent from the home. Sexual assault and/or rape. Hunger. Addiction. Racism.

According to Dr. Nadine Burke Harris, a pediatrician who serves as the first Surgeon General of California, practitioners now have a more meaningful way to measure the prevalence of trauma in the lives of children. The Adverse Childhood Experi-ences (ACEs) questionnaire asks about ten categories of events or conditions that shape not only our physical development, but our learning as well.[1] The higher the ACEs score, the more compounded the trauma. Someone carrying a score of four or more is at an increased likelihood of illness and negative life outcomes. It is estimated that approximately one in eight people in the United States is living with an ACEs score of four or more, disproportionately girls and other students vulnerable to school pushout. Dr. Burke Harris found that her "patients with four or more ACEs were 32.6 times as likely to have been diagnosed with learning and behavioral problems."[2]

Black and Brown girls disproportionately experience many of the incidents and conditions surveyed by the tool, including housing instability, hunger, parental substance use disorder, and childhood sexual assault (CSA), as well as the big one that is not on this tool, historical trauma. In her discussion of responses to chronic stress, Dr. Burke Harris has described those that are maladaptive, meaning that instead of "helping [one] thrive and survive, the response made things much, much worse," so that "early exposure often led not only to irreversible developmental changes but, eventually, to death."[3]

Maladaptive classrooms, those punitive learning environments that have emerged in response to the prevailing racialized gender bias that disproportionately criminalizes Black and Brown girls, may not often lead to death, but they do fan the flames of fear that trigger toxic stress. Too much stress causes problems in physical development and in the ability to function normally.

Why is it especially important to measure ACEs for Black and Brown girls? It's not about being intrusive or mapping the pain of students in order to support assumptions about the degree of dysfunction in any given household or community. Mapping ACEs can help educators build a more robust and expansive infrastructure to provide healing opportunities for girls who disproportionately experience harm. It helps to explain problematic behaviors, sure, but it's also a foundation for training, climate cultivation, and activities that can facilitate healing. Knowing, for example, that 70 percent of girls of color in a given classroom have ACEs scores of four or more can help the educator structure approaches to teaching that include opportunities to pause for breathing and guided movement, meditation, healthy snacks, or prompts that help a student connect subject matter with her own road to recovery. It also provides a foundation for investments in staff and faculty and for partnerships with agencies that can help develop learning environments in which our girls understand and, more important, *feel* that someone cares about their well-being.

The work of the educator, and anyone seeking to be responsive to trauma among girls of color, is to create and elevate opportunities that support a more rigorous interrogation of the culture, the policies, and the internalized ideas informing what we teach and how we teach it. Screening students for ACEs without developing a coordinated response would be empty, and in fact, irresponsible. It is important to note that, as with all equity efforts, data collection is only *the first step* in understanding issues associated with misbehavior and conflict among girls of color—not the only step. Developing relationships and other resources to add context to the numbers and then developing a plan to respond to the trauma girls face—both are essential. Once girls tell us what has happened to them (which may take time and relationship building), we need to be prepared to respond.

Dr. Burke Harris calls for adults who work with children to become "ACE-buffers."[4] But becoming an effective buffer is harder than it sounds. Educators and students must have a foundation of trust in order for there to be an authentic exchange that can (1) handle the honesty that often accompanies the disclosure of adversity and trauma, (2) respond with an appropriate facilitation of healing for individual students, and (3) inform the creation of conditions that normalize schools as locations where everyone feels safe. For girls with histories of trauma, it is important that they know we care before they open themselves to caring about what we know.

Oakland Uplifts African American Female Excellence

In 2016, the Oakland Unified School District in California officially launched the African American Female Excellence (AAFE) program to respond to the needs of Black girls in grades pre-K through 12. A district-led effort to support Black girls, AAFE became an important convener of training sessions to support educators and to design an infrastructure of investments that uplift and organize for the well-being of Black girls citywide. Its leader, Nzingha Dugas, was no stranger to building and growing programs for girls in the Bay Area, and she immediately set out to listen to girls in the district. She heard about sex trafficking, substance use, violence, and erasure (denial of contributions or failure to be included in public discourses). This led to the realization that girls in Oakland need their stories amplified, and ultimately to an annual citywide conference where girls could come together and share their experiences in schools, right there in the community.

"We have to speak our truths," Ms. Dugas said to me as she was describing the need for trauma-responsive programs to recognize the ways in which social structures contribute to risks

facing Black girls and the women who work with them. We are
resilient in the embrace of our sisters, so AAFE developed the
conference as a way to scale up the process for making these
truths more widely known.

The first AAFE Black Girl Power Conference was held on the
campus of Mills College where hundreds of Black girls in Oakland partnered with Black women and others to exchange strategies to achieve educational equity and justice. Young community
leaders shared their observations, and older women offered life
lessons.

It was not an empowerment conference, because as we engage
in education as freedom work, we recognize that we are not the
saviors of Black girls. Rather we try to increase their ability to
advocate for themselves in a way that they can sustain hence-
forth. The choice to focus on "power" is essential to this conversation about sustainability. For so many girls, power is perceived as
an individual assertion, as aggression or dominance, rather than
as our community's rhythm section. A school district–led effort,
this conference locates power in a collective *learning*. In sessions
throughout the day, girls and young women were reminded how
to harness their collective spirit of resistance and their historical
knowledge to fuel the "magic" that the world recognizes in Black
girls. There was some profanity. Tears were abundant. Responding to trauma is often a little messy. But it was powerful.

AAFE leads a weekly class with middle school girls that offers
an opportunity for them to build community in an affinity space
while honing research and advocacy skills that will serve them
well as scholars. In 2019, I observed a seventh-grade class that
provided an impressive display of co-constructed leadership in

learning. Two girls stood at the front of the class, one serving as a
scribe, the other as a facilitator. The word "condone" was written
on the white board, along with the "proverb of the week," a quote
from the writing of Alice Walker, who was also their Woman of
the Week. The two students held roll call and kept track of student offerings to the learning community through "cowries," or
tally marks to denote participation. They also led the practice of
collecting a word or phrase from each girl in the room to establish the shared values for class that day.

"One mic, one voice.
Love one another.
Encouragement.
Creativity.
Be responsible.
Caring.
Teamwork.
Be bold.
Collaboration.
No put downs.
Kindness.
Participation.
Fairness.
Respectful."

Then they recited each word in unison.
Planning for their field trip to Washington, DC, for a visit to
the National Museum of African American History and Culture, the girls separated into groups and developed a primary

research question. As they worked diligently, I realized that girls who had been labeled as "fighters" or who had a history of being perceived as disruptive in the learning space were working together with their instructors to learn participatory research methods—advancing skills that would make them better facilitators of culture and community.

I later learned that the girl who had been serving as a facilitator once had an incident in the classroom that she thought would end her participation in the program. She'd cursed out a teacher, which she understood was a violation of the trust established among the group. But instead of being removed from the class, she was counseled by one of the adults in the program to take accountability for her actions and actively repair her relationship with the group. The girl wrote a letter to Ms. Dugas, explaining that she had been having a bad day, that she knew she had violated the rules of the community, but that she hoped to return to the class.

"We didn't hesitate to bring her back in," Ms. Dugas explained. "This work is about forgiveness."

Empathy Matters

Marissa was a student in an alternative school in Oakland. She had been raped. She internalized the assault, often referring to herself as a "sinner." Her teachers and mentors noticed that she had become increasingly distrustful of them. They wondered what happened, and found that her stress was starting to overwhelm her. As an undocumented immigrant, Marissa was already unsure of her relationship with school when federal efforts to eliminate DACA* threatened her future in the United States. Fearful of deportation, Marissa stopped attending school. But her community of educators would not let her fail. They kept calling, kept reaching out, until they were able to place her in another school—one that would provide counseling and accelerated credit accrual, and that would hold her hand through her healing process. Instead of being dropped for being truant, the sense of urgency to respond to her *increased* because of the conditions surrounding her absence from school. Rape and the threat of deportation are scary for anyone, let alone a sixteen-year-old. Educators and educational policy makers must build learning spaces that are *responsive* to trauma, rather than neglectful or facilitative of it.

Research has shown that individuals who have some life experience with adversity also have an increased capacity for empathy for others in similar situations. We know this intuitively. That's why, when asked, girls of color express how important it is for them to have teachers and program facilitators who hail from conditions similar to theirs. The amygdala, the portion of the brain that can lead a student to respond to a perceived threat or harm with "fight, flight, or freeze," is shown to function at reduced integrity among those who experience a chronic lack of empathy. So, in order to resist our human urge to be egocentric,

---

* DACA, Deferred Action for Childhood Arrivals, is a federal program for eligible youth offering relief from deportation. The program, created in 2012 under the administration of President Barack Obama, came under fire by the Trump administration in 2017.

we have to *practice* being empathetic. We literally have to meditate on it.

A study by researchers at the Center for Investigating Healthy Minds at the Waisman Center at the University of Wisconsin–Madison found that compassion can be trained and learned by adults—and that practicing an empathetic mind-set can facilitate a change in worldview and the actions that follow.[5] The researchers understood the implications for students. One of them, Richard Davidson, said, "Compassion and kindness training in schools can help children learn to be attuned to their own emotions as well as those of others, which may decrease bullying."[6]

But what about teachers and school leaders who lack empathy for girls of color, those who have been conditioned to see children—particularly Black girls—as problematic?

In *Girlhood Interrupted: The Erasure of Black Girls' Childhood*, researchers at the Center on Poverty and Inequality of the Georgetown University Law School found that, compared with white girls of the same age, African American girls in a nationwide survey were perceived to "need less nurturing, less protection, to be supported less, to be comforted less, to be more independent, to know more about adult topics, and to know more about sex."[7] The disparity in perception begins when girls are as young as five and peaks when they are between the ages of ten and fourteen. While this "adultification" is not news to many African American women, it does provide an opportunity to explore the implicit biases that prevent many of us from recognizing and responding to trauma among Black girls. Participants in the study were described as "predominantly white

(74 percent) and female (62 percent). Thirty-nine percent were 25–34 years old . . . sixty-nine percent held a degree beyond a high school diploma."[8] The authors of the study noted,

> If authorities in public systems view Black girls as less innocent, less needing of protection, and generally more like adults, it appears likely that they would also view Black girls as more culpable for their actions and, on that basis, punish them more harshly despite their status as children. Thus, adultification may serve as a contributing cause of the disproportionality in school discipline outcomes, harsher treatment by law enforcement, and the differentiated exercise of discretion by officials across the spectrum of the juvenile justice system.[9]

Because oppression can also be internalized, many adults of color also participate in the age-compression imposed upon Black girls specifically, and on other girls of color, rendering them vulnerable to harsher treatment in schools—at an age when they are particularly sensitive to external influences. Adultification can also result in an overall lack of patience or interest in exploring root issues with children when they make mistakes or behave in destructive ways—hallmarks of being a child.

Educators need to recognize trauma before they can respond to it. They have to know when a child has only "got her own." Reading the behaviors of Black and Brown girls as simply disruptive or responding to incidents of harm without recognizing them as symptoms of something we can mitigate is maladaptive.

Instead, schools must become places where educators teach less
with their own egos and more with their hearts and minds—
even their souls—in order to set conditions for safety that facilitate learning. To do otherwise is dangerous.

⌒

When Zariah was in the second grade, she was violently pulled
from her classroom after a minor disagreement with a classmate
prompted her teacher to intervene. A boy had given her a quarter, and then demanded it back. When she refused, believing
that the quarter was now hers, the boy called for the teacher.
The teacher also demanded that Zariah return the coin, so she
finally did, but she did not think it was fair. He'd given it to her;
she hadn't taken it. So she was upset about how the incident, and
her honor, were being characterized. Frustrated, she sat down at
her desk with force, accidentally knocking over a cup of building
blocks. The teacher dragged Zariah's desk from the classroom,
publicly shamed her, and left her outside the classroom—which
was actually outside, in the cold winter weather of Sacramento,
California, without her jacket or coat.

Unattended, Zariah left the school campus and, at age seven,
wandered over dangerous freeways and overpasses until she
reached an intersection where she thought it might be better to
"go to heaven right now." Thankfully, an adult intervened and
she was convinced to head toward home. Along the journey, her
family discovered her. As she described her thoughts to me, she
held on to a quiet reserve, standing in her truth that to be con-
stantly berated in school, to be assigned a "behavior problem"
she did not really have, and then to be unheard by authority
figures left her in a depression that was only made worse by a

second-grade teacher who Zariah believed "didn't like" her. Violence in school, especially by someone trusted to love and teach, has consequences. Zariah, at seven, contemplating suicide over abuse at school, speaks to the desire of all young people to have a safe space to learn and grow. Her experience shows how harmful it can be when we fail to make schools such a place. Her parents rightfully removed her from this school, placing her into a new one, where she could reclaim her identity as a scholar and welcomed member of a learning community.

When I asked her what made her new school a good place to learn, especially after the last one, she smiled and said, "I feel loved, and I can laugh."

To be responsive to trauma, schools have to demonstrate that no child is disposable. To *care* is not a passive or benign activity in the learning space. Girls (as with all children!) need to *feel* it. They need to breathe it. The care, as publicly expressed in the policies, practices, and conditions we create to establish schools as locations for healing, has to acknowledge that trauma is not something to bury. It is something to talk about, to sing about, and to center as a key informant in the pedagogy—and andragogy—that governs what happens in schools.

According to the Child Mind Institute, signs of lasting trauma among children may include:

- increased thinking about suicide, death, or mortality;
- difficulty sleeping and eating;
- unexplained irritability and anger;
- difficulty focusing on projects, schoolwork, or conversations; and
- increased separation anxiety.[10]

Sometimes these symptoms are not evident until three to six months after an event.

What educators believe about their students determines how they engage with their students. Schools that create trauma-informed, healing-responsive conditions for girls of color do so by preparing their educators to respond to these symptoms with empathetic classroom management. These strategies shift the mind-set of educators to recognize that one of the strongest predictors of classroom behavior is the quality of a student's relationship with her teacher.[11] Researchers have found that when educators respond to misbehavior with less punishment and more empathy, as by rearranging seating or simply talking with students directly about their actions, suspension rates decrease and students' respect for authority increases.[12]

Research on empathetic (or empathic) discipline supports attacking one of the most difficult elements of school-to-confinement pathways for girls: racialized gender bias. According to Jason Okonofua and other researchers involved in a study on the matter:

> The empathic-mindset intervention did not attempt to teach teachers new skills for interacting with students or introduce new policies for how to discipline students. . . . The intervention simply encouraged teachers to view discipline as an opportunity to facilitate mutual understanding and better relationships and empowered teachers to do so in a manner effective for them and their students. . . . Punitive mindsets about discipline serve as a critical barrier to better teacher-student relationships.[13]

If educators believe that girls who act out (or act *in*) are "troublemakers," they are more inclined to respond with punishment. However, like their excessively punitive counterparts, overly permissive environments can produce negative outcomes as well—and can result in teachers losing control of the classroom. If they understand that behaviors can be improved through relationships and respect, they respond with empathy. According to Okonofua and his colleagues, the results of their experiment show "that teachers can be encouraged to take an empathic approach to discipline and that students report that such treatment motivates better behavior."[14]

"I like my teacher," Zariah said, speaking of her fifth-grade English teacher. "Schools should show you they care. My [new] school does this very well—like they provide people to talk to, and if you're feeling a certain way, go straight to them. They're comforting, and they make you feel that you can tell them anything and feel like you've been heard. . . . I feel better."

As she spoke, her wide grin revealed a row of silver braces. The warmth of her comfort blanketed not only her face, but her entire body. Her shoulders relaxed, her posture loosened, and her eyes lit up—matching her rediscovered interest in school.

Positive relationships are healing.

Teaching to the Oppression Is Traumatic

The intellectual, emotional, and psychological safety of girls of color in schools also includes teaching curricula and creating classroom conditions that are free from racism, sexism, homophobia, transphobia, and other forms of bias. A violent curriculum—one that triggers historical trauma by carelessly handling academic content—can be just as disruptive to learning as physical violence.

In Nashville, Tennessee, eleventh- and twelfth-grade girls shared a story about how a racial climate produced by the toxic politics of white supremacy had created triggering conditions for their learning in school.

"What happened?" I asked.

A white classmate had made them feel unsafe and jeopardized their trust in school as a safe space for them to learn. He had made several racially charged remarks, using the word *nigger* while holding a whip. When confronted, he dismissed the act as a joke. To these African American girls, it was a threat of violence. Regardless of his intent or judgment, which was poor, the outcome was harmful. Yet for weeks afterward, to secure *his* physical safety in school, the offending student was escorted to and from class each day by the school resource officer.

The girls were livid. They were visibly triggered by the idea that he could verbally assault them and get away with it. His sense of safety seemed more important than theirs.

When I asked how the school could have responded differently, many of the girls shrugged. Then one girl rolled her eyes and said, "He should have been suspended."

"What could happen *other than suspension*?" I asked.

I wanted to take suspension off the table, since the isolation of anyone allows wrongdoing and oppression to fester.

"I guess we could talk about it," another student suggested.

The girls intuitively understood that talking it out might be a way to resolve conflict. "We need a sense of community," said one.

"We all need to learn more about the Black experience—beyond slavery," said another.

"And we just need more Black teachers," one student stated. "Teachers need to build relationships."

There it was! Unprompted. Relationships and an increased capacity to contextualize—and appropriately historicize—the institution of slavery as neither the beginning nor the end of Black identities. These Black girls were longing for a curriculum that incorporated their histories, interpretations, and contributions to American narratives. Other students need this too. The patriarchal, heteronormative, Eurocentric nature of most pedagogical approaches and academic content prepares children of color, girls, and people who express gender and sexuality along a continuum, for a lifelong narrative of exclusion and marginalization. They either do not see themselves reflected at all in the primary content, or they see themselves as footnotes in a dominant narrative about American exceptionalism, one that minimizes the ways in which people, together, have survived some of this nation's greatest tragedies and achieved its extraordinary victories.

"Oh, the violence that comes with erasure!" exclaimed Brittany Brathwaite, organizing and innovation manager for Girls for Gender Equity in New York and a lead author of the 2017 report *The School Girls Deserve: Youth-Driven Solutions for Creating Safe, Holistic, and Affirming New York City Public Schools.*

"[In schools] you are not *here*," she continued. "'We are going to teach you about other people, about other people's history, other people's experiences. You don't exist.' Many youth of color are like, 'We go to school, but we're not *in* school'—meaning, we're not in any part of the school outside of our mere presence there. Like, teachers don't look like us. Teachers don't teach us about us, and when they do, they make it an elective. You can elect to teach about Black people. You can elect to teach about queer people, but school is not about *you*."[15]

Typically, "culturally inclusive" content does little more than present tertiary discussions about people of color, mostly celebrating male leaders of racialized social movements. Sometimes a narrative is offered to engage students, but it is rarely presented as central to understanding what is considered *essential* knowledge. As Brittany said, it's something students can choose to learn, or not. Curricula that offer only a smattering of narratives about Black and Brown suffering actually reinforce the dominant narrative of white supremacy. While rooted in historical fact, they often perpetuate a narrative of white dominance that primes students to view people of color as inherently subservient, overpowered by white "greatness." They're primed to believe that they need to be saved, or at least that their ancestors did.

Language in history texts often reflects a colonizer's perspective. White people are "settlers" who "discover" lands that have already been inhabited for thousands of years. Black people are seldom mentioned except in the context of slavery, and even then their freedom is presented as an outcome of Abraham Lincoln's generosity and the fruit of other white people's labor and sympathy. People of color are falsely presented as less powerful, less astute, less advanced, and less progressive than Europeans. Oppressive themes are woven into lesson plans about people of color without many educators even being aware that they are exacerbating the prevailing consciousness and conditions that prime girls of color for dismissal, underperformance, or criminalization. Stated more simply, the savior mentality is a tool of oppression.

In her article "Waiting for Superwoman," Amy Brown—a self-described white woman from a middle-class background—describes how perceptions about conditions in African American and Latinx homes shape pedagogical practices that reinforce a neoliberal narrative of white saviorism. She writes:

> Not unlike the antebellum White proselytizers who expanded the influence of the church by teaching Black slaves, whom they called the "heathen of the new world," to read so that they could read the bible and one day find salvation (Woodson, 1919), or the U.S. Federal Government and Bureau of Indian Affairs 19th and 20th century projects of Native American assimilation through schooling (Lomawaima, 1995, Farb, 1991, Hunt, 2012), a missionary zeal lies behind much of the discourse of urban alternative certification programs, and many of the ideals of young teachers in urban classrooms. These programs, through "populational reasoning," can serve to normalize young predominantly White middle-class teachers while constructing "urban" or "at-risk" students as an "Other" who needs to be saved (Popkewitz, 1998).[16]

This approach to teaching is why, for so many youth of color and their families, education has functioned as part of the tapestry of harm in their lives, rather than part of the fabric of healing. For centuries, marginalized communities have believed education to be a tool for liberation and resistance to oppression, but they never forget the historically complicated nature of getting and using this crucial tool. It's a challenging narrative, a script that is especially hard to rewrite when educators fail to do the necessary work on their own implicit biases.

In Berkeley, California, I encountered a middle school teacher from a private school who, on the first day of school, asked her students to "imagine that they were slaves" and to write a narrative based upon that experience as part of an introduction to teaching about the global trafficking of African people and their labor between the seventeenth and nineteenth centuries. While giving the instructions, the teacher said offhandedly, "Now remember, slaves were *property*, so write from that perspective." Technically, she was not wrong. Enslaved African people were indeed recorded as property. However, her remark triggered the large collective of non-Black children to nervously trade glances and gaze at the few African American children in the class.

A white child leaned over to an African American girl and said, "I'm going to misspell words on purpose because these slaves had no education."

The girl stopped writing and frowned.

The teacher had used oppressive language by referring to enslaved Africans as property without a basic discussion about racial oppression and power—and thus had created a classroom that reinforced notions of white supremacy and made her Black students uniquely vulnerable.

By not establishing the role of structural and cultural oppression as part of her teaching, and by assigning an essay that would invite students to vent their own stereotypes and biases without proper facilitation and discussion, she unwittingly perpetuated these oppressions for her students of color. Her lesson plan failed to acknowledge that it was often *illegal* for Black people to study, that enslaved Africans caught *attempting* to read or write were punished, and that they were routinely whipped and chained for the express purpose of dehumanizing them.

The Black girl who was most visibly upset about the assignment remained a high performer in this teacher's class, but she never developed a positive relationship with her teacher that could have helped shield her from the dismissive response she received when she voiced dissent. She felt pain from knowing that her teacher, knowingly or subconsciously, expressed white supremacist leanings.

In a meeting with the teacher, we discussed these dynamics. She insisted that her intention was to make sure her students could talk about difficult things. A bit defensively, she said, "I know these are hard issues, but we have to talk about them. This is how we will prevent things like Charlottesville from happening."*

I agreed. We do have to talk about them. It's not that students from historically marginalized, culturally and linguistically diverse communities can't learn about racially or culturally charged historical events. But if schools are to be locations where we do no further harm, these lessons require preparation, an understanding that historical trauma is about a collective,

---

* In 2017, a white nationalist rally occurred in Charlottesville, Virginia, prompting student- and community-led protests. One of the white supremacists attacked the protesters by driving his car into the crowd, killing Heather Heyer. Donald Trump, as president of the United States, responded sympathetically to the white nationalists, prompting criticism from opponents of racial violence and hate speech.

unresolved grief. Addressing biases that work against our ability to recognize and respond to trauma is essential to repair the relationship between educational systems and people of color.

This teacher thought she could "save" her students from participating in discrimination by asking them to complete a fundamentally flawed assignment. Instead, the assignment revealed a failure to prepare for the safety of all her students, particularly those of color in this discussion. She admitted that she "never would have thought to do this assignment [this way] on the Jewish Holocaust" because it is commonly understood as a deeply emotional subject for those whose forebears suffered in it.

Educators, like everyone else, have to do the hard work to confront biases that shape how knowledge is transferred. I casually asked the girl, six months after the incident, if she ever thinks about this first lesson of the school year.

"No," she replied forcefully. "I don't like her, though. I don't trust her."

Building schools that nourish the soul requires us to respond to the *whole* child, to consider not just academic needs, but also the need to create a space where girls of color *feel* safe. Girls of color should perform well *because* of the conditions in their learning environment, not *in spite of* them.

The criminalization of girls of color is intertwined with structural and cultural oppressions that produce individual and collective trauma. Educational content that reinforces a "savior complex"* triggers the historical traumas that girls of color

---

* A "savior mentality" is one that emphasizes saving a person from a condition of harm, real or perceived.

experience when they're perceived as ungrateful for the interventions of well-meaning educators who want to "save" kids,
and fail to secure conditions for their intellectual and emotional
well-being. Black and Brown girls who don't see themselves in
the curriculum, in narratives that aren't as diverse as their communities are in real life, detach from the material and come to
view education as a game rather than as a tool for their freedom.
Fortunately, there are ways to better shape curriculum and to
make the experience of school culturally relevant to students.

In Nigeria, for example, there is a model wherein educators are
recruited from the ethnic communities in which they would be
teaching. The focus is on developing organic leadership to ensure
that emergent teachers are equipped with "transferrable leadership skills to effect change beyond the classrooms in the communities we serve."[17]

In Lagos, I had the opportunity to meet with Folawe Omikunle, CEO of Teach for Nigeria, the nonprofit agency leading
the work of seeking to improve educational outcomes for Nigeria's most marginalized children. In this meeting, she said their
teachers overwhelmingly share the cultural norms and values of
those they are tasked to educate.

According to Ms. Omikunle, students take ownership of their
learning when schools provide an affirmation of their humanity.
Teachers, then, show care first and foremost. The group's goal,
she said: "I *care* about you. I *love* you, and I *want* you to learn."

This attitude doesn't happen by accident. I wanted to know
more about how her agency recruits to increase the capacity and
sustainability of educational leadership. I asked, "What is your
primary messaging to get this done?"

"We have a mixed recruitment pipeline; we recruit nationally and locally. Our messaging has focused on saying, 'Let us look inward for our own solutions in order to push forward as a nation.' In our year one, we led a national campaign drive that focused on recruiting teacher leaders to rewrite the narrative, and then this year, our messaging has focused on the need to get to our vision through collective leadership and effect."

I wondered how and why people are drawn to the program, to teaching in these communities. Is it because they need the experience, or are they drawn to teach children from their own ethnic group?

"They are drawn to the opportunity to be part of a movement that is teaching and impacting the lives of less privileged children in underserved communities from their state and country."

In Nigeria as in the United States and many other countries, money determines access to quality education. However, Ms. Omikunle highlighted the importance of their fellows being drawn to the idea that children who do not "have" are part of an extended community of people who do. The work of the teacher is not an act of charity, but about participating in the building of capacity. When responses to children in need are not placed explicitly within the context of historical racialized oppression, I wondered about the nature of educators' responses. But they, too, saw the need for specific tracking to address trauma among students.

"We have training designed to help our fellows identify trauma," Ms. Omikunle said. "We have also created a network of experts who are able to provide one-on-one advice and coaching on how to deal with traumatized children. The majority of our kids experience trauma."

Facilitating organic leadership is not just a good idea; it is a pedagogical thrust and praxis for liberation. The "violence of erasure" that Brittany from Girls for Gender Equity recognized requires both an acknowledgment of girls' trauma and a call to action. Purveyors of knowledge are some of the most powerful people in a society, and the way they share knowledge is inherently political. If guided by erasure and violence, their teaching practices will inevitably reinforce or increase existing oppression. This is why we have to screen and prepare educators to be a work in progress, rather than a stagnant representation of previous harms.

Teaching to the historical oppression means that the content and practices used to distribute knowledge systematically exacerbate and transfer the pain of those historical wrongdoings. Failing to engage in complete narratives about historical events is itself oppressive. Failing to explore the relevance of the Hindu-Arabic numerical system as the foundation for the positional notation we use in mathematics today, for example, is more than a minor omission. It's an expression of incompetence in evolving an inclusive worldview, one that improves our students' ability to compete in the global community. Teaching to historical oppression by ignoring the contributions of women and girls of color to society prolongs the unresolved transgenerational grief of racialized gender bias. It undermines the capacity for girls to realize their full potential as scholars.

This, too, is an act of violence.

⌢

"Who wants to buy my slave?" a student, a young white boy, asked his sixth-grade classroom.

His teacher, a thirty-year-old African American woman, remembers the sting of pain she felt when the words first started to make sense to her.

"What?" she remembers asking for clarity.

He repeated it: "Who. Wants. To. Buy. My. Slave?"

"Wait, did you just call my teacher your slave?" an African American boy asked.

"You need to sit down right now," she remembers saying. Meanwhile, she was thinking, *Is this really happening?*

Once the student sat down, this teacher acknowledged the increasing diversity in her Iowa community and recognized that this was a particularly difficult moment for the class. Though she viewed the act as a violent one, she took control of the situation by appealing to her students' sense of community and her leadership role in it.

"That just hurt my feelings," she finally said, looking deep into the eyes of the young white student who made the comment. "I never want any of you to feel the way I feel right now."

This was her first year teaching in a predominately white school, and she was concerned that this child could do this to her and "nothing will really come of it." She immediately reached out to her principal, who was also white, and to the boy's parents—ultimately receiving their support to respond as she saw fit.

She decided to try to maintain a positive relationship with the student, but she grappled with the shock of being referred to as a "slave" to her class by a student. In the seven years that she had been teaching, she had never encountered anything like this. It became clear to her that teachers must be prepared to host hard conversations in their classrooms if we are to co-construct safe spaces for learning and teaching.

"We must lead these conversations," she said. "It's part of it."

⌒

Healing from historical oppression and being cognizant of how it informs approaches to teaching and learning is a long-term process. Dr. Joy DeGruy, in *The Post-Traumatic Slave Syndrome*, states:

> It is no surprise that the teachers that have the most success working with many students of color emphasize building strong relationships based upon mutual trust and respect. . . . The legacy of trauma is reflected in many of our behaviors and our beliefs; behaviors and beliefs that at one time were necessary to adapt in order to survive, yet today serve to undermine our ability to be successful.[18]

This is our hard, ongoing work. We must begin by conducting an assessment of our curricula and lesson plans. We should be looking for themes and frameworks that present more-integrated narratives, for information that actually reflects the lived experiences of all our ancestors. People of African descent, as well as North, Central and South American Indigenous people and other people of color, co-constructed every discipline we study in the United States. The knowledge we share with students should reflect that, or, as Christopher Emdin shares, "If we are truly interested in transforming schools and meeting the needs of urban youth of color who are most disenfranchised within them, educators must create safe and trusting environments that are respectful of the students' culture. Teaching the neoindigenous requires recognition of the spaces in which they reside, and understanding how to see, enter into, and draw from these spaces."[19]

Mr. Green, a history teacher at a parochial high school in Oakland, California, understood this more than thirty years ago, when he began teaching Black history, becoming one of the first high school instructors to do so. For him, this journey began as a student in Vallejo, California, where Black Panther Party members would enter the school he attended, and teach students about their history. The Black Panther Party Community School design was led by Ericka Huggins, who described it as "a model for education that could be replicable anywhere."[20]

For Mr. Green, this meant starting a Black history course with an intention to transform students' understanding of their historical contributions to the development of the nation, but also of what their promise might be in the creation of society for generations to come.

"I wanted to inform the students and the school of the depth and breadth of the [African] Diaspora," he said. "I started the class in the middle of the crack epidemic, and a lot of people's understanding of Blackness was based on that. . . . I wanted to get kids to think differently. I sat in on Professor Oba T'Shaka's classes at San Francisco State University and at Berkeley High

School under Dr. Richard Navies. After that, I started the class here."

"What texts have you used?" I asked.

"When I first started, I used *From Slavery to Freedom*, and then I started using texts from my own library—[Frantz] Fanon, [Manning] Marable. We go to Marcus Books every year."

Marcus Books, a bookstore founded in 1960 by Drs. Julian and Raye Richardson, has been a community beacon for decades. Mr. Green uses the bookstore to demonstrate for students how culture is shaped by community, and vice versa—even in the era of extreme gentrification in Oakland.

"Once the churches started to disappear and the stories and grandparents started to die, I started to notice that my students responded to the material differently. They're not as responsive to the material because they're further removed from the movements."

Distance from an event can certainly dim one's sense of urgency, but his course provides a strong foundation for the contemporary movements that young people often struggle to contextualize. For example, the course has become a way to contextualize Black Lives Matter and the Occupy movement. Their understanding of the criminalization they experience in their communities becomes shaped by a learning space in which they explore and share their fears, questions, and concerns safely.

As part of finals, Mr. Green asked his students to prepare a short presentation on economic models associated with exploitation of Black labor. Students were free to explore various industries and models over time. Many focused broadly on capitalism, sometimes on specific industries, like cotton, marijuana, and prison. One morning, the first presenter was a tall, athletic teenager who spoke of Black economic infrastructures as she mapped the export of sugar and rum from the Caribbean. She was poised and confident. She was not the only student to show an intellectual curiosity about complex issues—with high buns and braids, and baby hairs laid, Black and Brown girls, as well as other students, were safely supported in a classroom adorned with African masks and figurines, posters of Billie Holiday, Marian Anderson, and Frederick Douglass, and *piles* of books about the African Diaspora. In every way, the students could know that they matter—intellectually, experientially, presentationally, and practically. Mr. Green's class hosts the conditions to support their learning.

That's definitely replicable—and should be, alongside courses that center the experiences of other people of color, part of a core curriculum.

Foundations for Transformation

For educators, addressing historical trauma can become an amorphous, hard-to-grasp ideal, if we let it. However, there are many concrete opportunities to respond to the way longstanding patterns of racialized gender oppression manifest today. For instance, policies or practices (like dress codes) that encourage adults to read and police the *bodies* of girls are rooted in the patriarchal practice of limiting or filtering the value of a woman's contributions through her physical presentation. Cultural and ethnic stereotypes also make policing bodies, clothes, and appearance a form of racial oppression.

In addition to assessing a school's core curriculum for opportunities to be responsive to its full student body, leaders of schools should conduct a complete racial and gender equity assessment of codes of conduct, classroom management expectations, and parental engagement guidelines. Race Forward: The Center for Racial Justice Innovation[21] and many schools offer guidelines for conducting this type of assessment. Guiding questions might include, but are not limited to:

- How will Black, Latinx, Indigenous, and other girls of color be positively and negatively affected by this issue?
- How are the experiences of girls and young women in various racial and social groups uniquely situated in relation to this policy/rule/proposal?
- How do we support cultural relations to education through this policy/rule/proposal?
- What data and other information do we need to form this policy/rule/proposal with consideration for racialized gender equity?
- Who is accountable for upholding racial and gender equity in this policy/rule/proposal?[22]

The ideal learning environment has educators who strive to become ACE buffers—forces to interrupt and counteract the harm from past trauma. There is a growing body of academic research on the effectiveness of interventions that explore and build from empathy. Many of these interventions fall under the umbrella of social-emotional learning (SEL). According to Jonathan Cohen, "Recent studies have shown that research-based social, emotional, ethical, and academic educational guidelines can predictably promote the skills, knowledge, and dispositions that provide the foundation for the capacity to love, work, and be an active community member."[23] SEL isn't about sacrificing or undermining the importance of academic content or curricula. It's about making our young people feel safe enough to learn.

Social, emotional, ethical, and academic education (SEEAE) is an emerging framework that acknowledges multiple ways of knowing. It is associated with four primary findings:

1. Social and emotional competencies are predictive of children's ability to learn and solve problems nonviolently.
2. Social and emotional capacities are as "brain-based" as linguistic and mathematical competencies.
3. The vast majority of children can learn to become socially and emotionally competent.
4. There are processes that characterize effective SEEAE efforts:

    a. Cultivating long-term educator-parent partnerships to create safe, caring, participatory, and responsive schools and homes.
    b. Purposely teaching children to be more socially, emotionally, ethically, and cognitively competent.[24]

Schools that prioritize SEL implement more responsive policies and practices. But these schools must also ensure that the norms they seek to establish among students do not reinforce negative stereotypes or bias against Black and Brown girls. This means SEL and other efforts that extend epistemology in the classroom must also unpack the biases that lead educators toward a goal of "fixing" student behavior rather than uplifting connections that provide maximum opportunity for trust, healing, and learning. They offer teachers a continuum of alternatives to punitive discipline that foster self-regulation and awareness. They help everyone "take a breath between verses," because it's those social-emotional skills that enable kids to adopt positive coping habits in response to trauma.

In partnership with The Mentoring Center, Girls, Inc., the Alameda County Office of Education, and the National Black Women's Justice Institute, I helped establish a pilot educational reentry program for girls, in Oakland, California, called EMERGE—Educating, Mentoring, Empowering and Reaffirming Our Girls for Excellence. In 2017, a group of girls from EMERGE participated in the first national conference on Chicana/Latina girls in the juvenile justice system. For some of the Brown girls in the program, this field trip was their first time witnessing Chicana/Latina women in power, women who looked like them and who were shaping their own destinies with grace, to a rhythm different from the hustle of the street.

Their eyes witnessed the giant altar at the front of the room, paying tribute to ancestors who were called to join us for the day. In calling the ancestors, the facilitators also called to the fore a need in one of our girls to tell her story. Just days before coming to this historic gathering, Esperanza had been jumped and violently robbed by a group of girls, who left her feeling vulnerable, angry, and possibly a bit embarrassed. Halfway through the conference, Esperanza began to assert the need to tell her story. She wanted to speak. And then she didn't. She felt nauseated. She felt anxious. Suddenly she started to breathe very heavily, tears starting to roll down her cheeks.

Falilah, the therapist who had been working with our girls, reached out and held her hand. Her classmate slowly rose from her seat to go behind Esperanza's chair. She gently grabbed handfuls of Esperanza's hair and began to braid. The wisdom of generations was embedded in her instinct to braid as a practice that might soothe Esperanza's anxiety.

"Breathe," Falilah said. "Say what you need to say to us. It's going to be okay."

And she did.

Together they were breathing to a tempo that would light a path to her own liberation, that would guide her journey past the ghosts that haunted her. In her private testimony, she was decolonizing her thinking about which stories were valid in the public domain, and which ones were not. She was healing so that she could learn what the elders and ancestors had to offer.

That's freedom work.

Practicing Awareness

Most pedagogical practices that profess to be trauma-informed now recognize that our brains are designed to respond to trauma in a manner that may have a negative impact on student learning. Yoga and mindfulness practices—intentional breathing, focused body movement, and other centering exercises to increase one's resilience to stress—are particularly well-suited for school. When offered in earnest and faithfully implemented, they provide girls of color with opportunities to de-escalate from triggers and focus on their capacity to learn. The Oakland-based Niroga Institute had developed a plan called Dynamic Mindfulness, which it says is "an evidence-based, trauma-informed stress resilience program [with] elements [that include] mindful movement, breathing practices, and centering practices . . . that can be implemented in the classroom in 5-minute to 20-minute sessions, three to five times a week."[25] Deepak Chopra invites us to understand this as "living in awareness," where a focus on breathing and the alignment of mind and body produces opportunities to reduce stress and discover truths about our intentions.[26] Meditation and yoga engage somatic responses to stress that can help students feel calmer. One Baltimore elementary school reported that its Mindful Moment Room eliminated the use of suspensions.[27]

In a Miami-based alternative school run by the Pace Center for Girls, meditation is offered to girls who need time to self-regulate and regroup after a conflict. When I visited the school, I checked out their meditation room. It's the size of a small conference room, lined with pillows and rugs, with soft lighting to facilitate calm. Other schools with girls who have significant histories of trauma, victimization, and school pushout create spaces in classrooms that serve a similar function. At EMERGE, we aimed to create a space for girls to breathe, to engage drama therapy and dance to process troubling incidents, or to use the arts and sports as a conduit for self-regulation and healing.

Practicing awareness or mindful meditation has been found to produce positive outcomes, particularly when used with other interventions. A randomized controlled trial in Canada found

that, relative to other children, those who received the SEL program with mindfulness:

1. improved more in their cognitive control and stress
   physiology;
2. reported greater empathy, alternative perspective-taking,
   emotional control, optimism, school self-concept, and
   mindfulness;
3. showed greater decreases in self-reported symptoms of
   depression and peer-rated aggression; and
4. were rated by peers as more prosocial, with increased
   peer acceptance (sociometric popularity).[28]

Mindfulness is not just a practice for the classroom; it can also
be practiced in community. For many girls of color who are in
communities experiencing transgenerational trauma, or trauma
that has been passed down in the family history, working with
families and community partners through mindful awareness
practices can mitigate the impact of this type of trauma.[29]

Being mindful is not always about silent reflection. While quiet, nonverbal modes are certainly appropriate for some scenarios,
blues women teach us that humming, singing, and other musical
vibrations are also somatic expressions that can soothe the spirit.
It creates the condition for healing by setting the intention to do
so. A 2016 phenomenological study by Gayle Flynn found that,
among "Black/African American, Latina/Hispanic American,
Native American" girls and those with "two or more racial identities combined," for those who have been labeled aggressive, belligerent, and troublemakers, "support programs that *specifically
address the attitudes of indifference and coldness toward other*

girls in educational settings could be instrumental in changing the girls' perceptions of consequences that currently don't really matter to them."[30] This is a *mindful* intervention that is *aware* of the negative energy that needs to be repurposed in order for girls to be brought in *closer*, to build relationships that dissolve the icy indifference that limits their capacity to build meaningful relationships. For girls who are survivors of trauma but hail from communities with few financial resources, school may be one of the only locations to address indifference and/or detachment, especially when that has been part of their resistance to harm.

According to Lillian Comas-Díaz and Beverly Greene, women of color also use spiritual strategies such as faith and religiosity to cope with spirit injuries and soul wounds. What's more, Shorter-Gooden (2004) identified African American women's internal coping mechanisms as "standing on shoulders"—that is, drawing strength from ancestors. Cultivating a positive self-image, spirituality, harmony, and collectivism may resonate with Black girls as well.[31] Hispanic and Latinx women, whose "coping styles emanate from a legacy of colonization, immigration, acculturation, and adaptations to diverse cultural contexts . . . may cope with assertiveness, anger, or defiance [while] less acculturated Latinas may resort to more traditional mechanisms of defense."[32] In short, culturally relevant mindfulness practices can support healing and awakening. Schools that demonstrate—in culture, curriculum, faculty, and extracurricular activities—the importance of historical legacies of women's resistance rooted in practicing awareness shift the narrative. They move from girls who've got their own, to girls who have a community, a squad. It's a matter of girls transforming from "have-nots" to "haves."

Individual strategies for de-escalation and self-regulation are helpful, but these and other studies suggest that approaches to supporting girls of color with histories of trauma must include efforts to understand and heal from collective historical and contemporary oppression *in order to* address emotional and/or behavioral responses to trauma.[33] For Black and Brown girls, a contextualization of their trauma in the lived experiences of their people is part of setting positive conditions for learning and for positive relationship-building in the school community.

A trauma-informed and healing-responsive space of learning, then, requires cultural competency and gender responsiveness that is rigorous and intersectional, that creates space for varying forms of the spiritual—a higher source, power, or purpose that can and often does play a role in a young woman's recovery. Years ago, I wrote a paper on sacred inquiry in participatory research with systems-involved Black girls. In it, I stated, "Sacred experience and theory guide human inquiry toward recognizing the richness of an authentic, participatory experience, where practitioners appreciate and love the participant, not just attempt to treat her."[34] This may not be overtly possible in public institutions prohibited from integrating the practices of any particular religion into the instruction. Still, the study of cultural elevations of spirit remains important. It's part of how girls of color understand that, because they're "fit to wear to a crown," they're never truly without love. It's how they understand and believe that they've got community.

Pedagogical practices that contribute to the erasure of these spiritual contexts can themselves trigger trauma. In the previous chapter, when Principal Patton from the public middle school in Ohio acknowledged that *advocacy* needed to be included in her consideration of corrective actions, she was underscoring the need for girls to heal from structures of oppression that reinforce their perception of school as part of the tapestry of harm. Supporting girls, particularly those who've experienced trauma, to advocate for themselves lets their education become an act of social justice. This in turn creates an opportunity for educators and others in the school community to be ACEs buffers by leading with empathy, building positive relationships with girls, and helping those girls to recognize and *realize* their identities as scholars.

To better work with girls of color who are survivors of trauma, educators and others in the school community must grapple with what it takes to be healing-responsive. They can begin by asking these questions:

1. How might what I'm teaching—or not teaching— participate in the oppression of my students?
2. How does my classroom pedagogy reflect my understanding of intersectionality?*
3. How does my classroom culture respond to harm as an exchange that can be remedied or resolved in community?
4. How can I better facilitate conversations, breathing exercises, and quiet moments for meditation/reflection that provide my student community with an opportunity to safely interrogate difficult, potentially triggering, subject matter?

---

* "Intersectionality" is a term coined by Kimberlé Crenshaw to capture a framework in critical race theory that explores relationships among multiple identities and institutions, individuals, conditions. See "Mapping the Margins: Intersectionality, Identity Politics, and Violence Against Women of Color," *Stanford Law Review* 43, no. 6 (July 1991): 1241–99.

The crux of responding to trauma among girls of color is *empathy*—the capacity to understand and vicariously experience conditions that affect another. When used with empathy, resources like the Delta Teacher Efficacy Campaign, a national collaboration between the Delta Research and Educational Foundation (DREF) and Delta Sigma Theta Sorority, Inc. to improve student achievement by investing in the efficacy of teachers will increase their capacity to engage strategies like HELPS (Hear, Empathize, Lessen, Plan, and Sustain) when girls exhibit disruptive behaviors in response to trauma.[35] Likewise, efforts such as the Trauma-Informed Schools Learning Network for Girls of Color,[36] launched by the Georgetown Center on Poverty and Inequality and the National Black Women's Justice Institute in 2018 as a free resource for schools, will have an even greater impact on teachers' capacity to be part of girls' tapestry of healing. Schools that help a girl discover her own power become conduits for learning; those that suppress her will and her capacity, by failing to guide her healing from trauma do the opposite.

Robust training, staffing, retention efforts, and professional development require a significant investment of time and money. These resources are essential for schools, districts, and policy makers seeking to become more trauma-informed and healing-responsive. However, beneath it all must be the *intent* to shift the prevailing consciousness about Black girls and other girls of color so that their pain is recognized and their narratives are included in our collective learning in schools. Them that's got shall have—community.

And that's free.

Interlude

"I Want a Badass Girl"

One of the things that helped me as a middle schooler was that I was able to take metal shop. At school, being able to take metal shop added to the substance of who I was; it added to the strength. For me to be able to know how to use heavy machinery and build things out of metal—that supported my self-esteem.

Ultimately, I see a foundational piece of the work that I do as telling girls that we've been lied to. For thousands of years, we have been lied to. Our true purpose is so different from what we are living and what we have lived—particularly in the United States. Ultimately, it's about deciding collectively (as the school or other community), what we want to be. Not only looking at your students, but looking at your own granddaughters, your own daughters, whatever girls are in your life . . . How do we support a strong, self-advocating young person who can go to her own resources before going off and giving up her power to someone else?

When you see a girl who is challenging, who is pushing back, who is about to get on your last nerve in your classroom, how do you grab that strength and say, "Hold on. Can we shift that energy?"

That's a big part of the work that I do. We're building each girl's voice. We're supporting and facilitating the empowerment and development of her own, original voice. We have decided that a self-advocating, leadership-holding girl is someone we want.

If it seems she has those qualities, how do you redirect her energy and redevelop her fire? The fire is the *ganas*, her "will"—her will to live, her will to survive, her will to connect with all that has been given to her by all of her ancestors to move forward, her will to move forward when everybody seems against her. That's where we have to be realistic. Our girls—all they are is fire. If you get close to them, you're going to get burned.

They might say, "Who do you think you are? Why are you trying to get close to me? You think you know my life?"

Some of those girls have so much fire, all they have is rage. As adults in a community, a society, or a district, we can begin by just going back to the basic question—what has happened to you?—while acknowledging those specific, positive skills that we want for the girls to survive.

I think it's about the spirit of the work. What is a positive, powerful girl to you?

I want a badass girl, a *chingona*, who stands up for herself and others if she needs to, and who has the language to do it, the ability to do it. If she wants to go to college, I want to give her access to every university she wants. She can dream big, but she has to be *supported* to dream big. . . . What are the youth saying they want to be? When she shines and shows critical thinking and is challenging, let's not call the school resource officer and get her arrested. Let's take a minute and have that extra support system.

Sara Haskie Mendoza
National Compadres Network
New Mexico

Track 3
Cell Bound Blues

Removing Police from Schools

Tell me, what have I done?
>   —*Gertrude "Ma" Rainey, "Cell Bound Blues"*
>   *(Paramount Records, 1924)*

"Imagine schools without police officers in them," I said to a group of girls in Alabama who had assembled for a focus group that I was co-leading with my colleague Rebecca.

My invitation to the girls, whose skin tones reflected a spectrum of gradient browns, was politely declined. A few of the girls looked back at me with blank stares or confusion.

"No, seriously," I tried again. "Close your eyes and imagine a school where there is no law enforcement officer present."

This time, all of the girls refused. I searched their faces, looking for a reason for their lack of participation in this exercise. Then, finally, one of the girls spoke up.

"If there's no police," she said, "then who will keep us safe?"

My mind ticked through the myriad ways in which to create safety without the daily presence of police in schools, but I said none of them. Surveillance had become such a normalized part of these girls' lives that they could not—or were unwilling to—imagine an alternative scenario. To them, police officers (at least the ones inside schools) were supposed to be implementers of safety, people who would protect them from harm. So, even though—as they would later admit—they also understood that law enforcement in their school was not *inherently* beneficial to them, they had trouble, at that moment, articulating a form of school safety that didn't require a police escort.

I was now the one confused.

What is happening to the imagination of our children? I wondered.

The problem with a school safety strategy reliant on the presence of law enforcement is that it relies on a fabricated construct of safety in the first place. The goal of this chapter is not to paint law enforcement with a single, disparaging brush stroke. There are certainly officers who uphold fundamental values often associated with a life in public service, and who tirelessly give of themselves, working in schools and communities in ways that reflect a basic human decency and commitment to equal justice.

These officers volunteer their time, go beyond the call of duty to see Black and Brown girls as human beings, and work to support their well-being. Sometimes they behave as "big brothers" or "stand-in mothers" for girls in crisis, using their own personal resources to protect girls on the margins of society from harm. But in their positive interactions with students, they are not necessarily *policing*. They are deploying their own brands of compassion and social-emotional skills that they may have acquired from any number of experiences. They are drawing on their *humanity* in order to form healthy relationships with students. They are also using the tremendous discretion granted to them as members of law enforcement to provide resources to girls who have been otherwise outcast. In other words, they choose to lead with the qualities that make them good youth development professionals, not necessarily officers of the law. While that is commendable, it's also the problem. There is *so much* discretion in school policing work that those officers who openly or implicitly harbor animosity for girls of color are *also* left to their own devices, and that can facilitate harm.

In a conversation about how he makes decisions, one school law enforcement officer said, "I haven't had any specific training [specific to girls of color]. . . . I rely on the common sense God gave me."[1]

When I heard that, I couldn't help but cringe. "Common sense" is subjective and often developed by those in positions of power, rather than by those who have faced historical oppression. If a dominant narrative presents Black and Brown girls as salacious and problematic, then to *enforce* those misunderstandings with badge and gun can be catastrophic. #SayHerName.[2]

Safety is co-constructed, not implemented. No one and no thing can be *brought in* to generate safety. Safety must be developed by the individuals and institutions *together*. No one entity can ensure safety because no one entity alone is responsible for everything that could cause harm or protect someone from it.

Moreover, police officers are particularly ill-equipped to lead efforts that produce safety *in schools*, because they tend to respond to danger with the same tools used for oppression—intimidation, force, arrest, and violence.[3] These methods don't facilitate safety in schools. At times police may need to be called to remove a dangerous person, but their continuous presence has not been proven to prevent violence, nor do they by themselves generate safety for girls of color or any other students.

According to the National Association of School Resource Officers (NASRO), "School based policing is the fastest-growing area of law enforcement."[4] We have grown afraid of our children. Today 30 percent of public primary schools and 58 percent of public secondary schools have at least one school resource officer (SRO) on campus at least once a week. Forty-five percent of primary schools and 72 percent of secondary schools have security staff of some kind on campus.[5] In the 2013–14 academic year, more than 82,000 public schools throughout the United States had a police officer or guard on campus, but those with a white student population of 96 percent or higher (7,280 of 84,000 public schools) were much less likely to engage such personnel.[6]

The increase of policing in public schools, where most students of color are enrolled, has become part of the "safety" culture in education.[7] White students are less likely than students of color to meet law enforcement in school, and when they do, their experiences are quite different. In predominantly white schools (96 percent or more), law enforcement is more likely to participate in noncriminalizing activities with students, such as identifying problems and proactively seeking solutions, training teachers and staff in school safety and crime prevention, and teaching law-related courses for students. By comparison, in schools where less than half of the student population is white, law enforcement emphasizes training in crime prevention, but seldom does more.[8] These schools are preparing children of color, including a disproportionate number of Black and Brown girls, to be cell bound.[9]

Despite the increasing carceral influence, however, students do not report feeling safer in schools. In fact, as reporting on acts of violence by law enforcement against communities of color continues to grow, students increasingly express a *lack* of trust in police officers connected to their schools.[10] According to scholars who have studied student attitudes toward law enforcement, "public confidence in the police impacts the ability of the police to control crime because people who distrust the police are unlikely to report crimes or cooperate with police officers."[11] While there is still more research to be done on interactions between law enforcement and girls of color, broader studies have found that police presence in schools may have an impact on blatant acts of criminality but does little to change students' participation in covert delinquent activity or their sense of safety.[12] Indeed, according to criminologist Arrick Jackson,

> Police in schools may provide a psychological benefit for administrators, staff, parents, and the adult public; however, their presence may pose a psychological threat to students, who may view police as a threat to their freedom to move about, have open conversations, and experiment in legal activities that may be socially unacceptable to police and administrators.[13]

Teachers also recognize the problematic nature of a growing police presence in schools. Attorney Aaron Sussman stated that students in New York City were likely to see officers as "often belligerent, aggressive, and disrespectful" and that teachers, too, were increasingly aware of the violent ways in which they would interact with students. Calling officers "aggressive" and "combative" with students, 64 percent of the teachers found that school officers "never or rarely make the students feel safe."[14] These findings are part of a growing trend of criminalization that has contributed to racial disparities among girls.

⌒

In 2017, twelve-year-old Mariana Benton fought with another student in her Dallas, Texas, school. A school resource officer stepped in to break up the fight, which he did successfully. However, once the girls were separated, Marianna was lifted in the air by this officer and forcefully slammed to the ground.[15] Her hundred-pound sixth-grade body lay motionless on the floor, and video of the incident went viral.

"The officer came and grabbed me and body-slammed me," Marianna said. "He pepper-sprayed me in the eyes, and I couldn't open my eyes because it was burning me."

She was later diagnosed with a broken clavicle, which some in the community declared she "deserved." Violence against Black and Brown girls is often interpreted as deserved without consideration for the original conflict or recognition that these are children.

"No," her mother, Alma Valadez, stated on the news. "She's a twelve-year old girl . . . she did not deserve that."[16]

School resource officers themselves recognize the limitations of attempting to be part of the tapestry of healing when their institution has historically been associated with harm in communities of color. The study by the Georgetown Law Center on Poverty and Inequality and the National Black Women's Justice Institute, focusing on interactions between girls of color and school-based law enforcement, found that school resource officers acknowledged that working in schools required them to forge relationships with students—something that generally police are not *trained* to do. The researchers found that, while police officers have increased their interactions with girls of color, they do not receive training to specifically respond to the needs of these girls in their schools. One school resource officer stated:

> Girls of color are often perceived to be a certain way; they are perceived as lower-class, violent. If a girl of color challenges authority, it is deemed unacceptable. When girls don't fall in line, they get labeled as acting out. Black girls and women are quickly labeled as "crazy" or [having] an "attitude" because they are more vocal. Also, sometimes in schools girls of color are dealing with trauma—especially in my city, the girls are exposed to and experience trauma—so they may act out because of the trauma that is going on at home, and officers will have no idea, and have no idea how to respond accordingly. . . . The SROs get sex-trafficking training, but that is only one aspect of this. There is much more that we are missing, and girls of color are treated differently and often introduced to the justice system because of it, because of our lack of training.[17]

Lack of training is an important service-preparation gap among law enforcement in schools, but if we are committed to transforming conditions in schools so they facilitate healing and freedom to learn for girls of color, then we have to challenge not only the outcomes of differential treatment, but also the foundations that produce it. Perhaps the most compelling argument for the removal of police from schools is a question we only partially acknowledge: what becomes of children raised by the carceral state in a culture of surveillance?

"I got my GED when I was in prison," a woman said, as she looked down at a blank paper in front of her.

I was sitting with formerly incarcerated women on an Indigenous People's reservation in one of the northernmost parts of California. I was there to talk to them about barriers to employment upon return to community, when the conversation turned to their educational experiences. Most of the women acknowledged that they received their GED when they were incarcerated, making the implicit connection with the pushout story that Indigenous girls experience in the face of poverty and marginalization.

"I mean, that's still pretty much the only opportunity we have in jail is to go to school," another woman offered.

"I've been to jail to go to school. I got 69 credits left. I'm busting my butt this year. I'm going to walk . . . I want my diploma," said another.

The question of what happens to girls and young women who come of age in carceral settings is somewhat rhetorical, but my conversation with the women on the reservation that day reminded me that while they are incarcerated, and when they come back, there is still a desire to complete their high school education. It is a drum that beats in their soul, and which can reverberate for generations.

Dehumanization of Girls of Color Fuels Overpolicing in Schools

In 1987, Darnell Hawkins challenged the assumption of normalcy about Black criminality in America. He presented several examples of how violence among Black communities is viewed as normal, due to the *frequency* with which Black crime is reported and to the relatively limited law enforcement and judicial responses to acts of violence in Black communities.[18] That Black and Brown girls disproportionately experience arrest in schools obscures the reality that most girls of color in schools do *not* commit crimes, are law- and rule-abiding scholars, and do not warrant being surveilled or criminalized. Black, Latinx, and Indigenous populations are overrepresented in carceral settings—and in schools run with a carceral influence. This fact has become conflated with the incorrect notion that these communities perpetrate most crimes or exhibit more criminal behaviors than their white counterparts. Black and Latinx girls, in particular, no matter what they do or don't do—are often associated in the public mind with criminality.

When teenage white males are arrested for the murder of schoolmates and teachers, newspapers and national magazines quickly discuss their mental health status or behaviors as lone actors—careful descriptors to keep them marked as unusual. Historically, these boys have been described as "quintessentially American," "skinny," "slight," "freckle-faced," and "intelligent but isolated." None of the national coverage has referred to these youth as "superpredators," "maggots," or "animals"—language that has been used when a violent crime is perpetrated by someone of African descent.[19]

The most dehumanizing fight students of color face is the one to reclaim their identities from the minds of adults who believe they're prone to *become* "animals," "superpredators," or gang-affiliated, perceptions that serve to rationalize law enforcement in schools. Sometimes these misperceptions and assumptions are expressed overtly, but often they come in the form of unconscious bias that shapes how adults interact with students. This can be all the more frustrating and confusing for young people to combat.

I once visited a school district in Missouri whose school-serving police agency had a habit of handcuffing Black girls (more than other girls) to calm them down. In an honest, sometimes contentious, exchange among the district superintendent, school administrators, and law enforcement, I suggested that school should be a place where everyone believes in the promise of all children. In a moment of frustration, an African American police officer folded his arms and glared at me from the back of the room. He boasted about believing that children in public schools lack the capacity to routinely behave long enough to become high performers, even bragging about his decision to send his own children to private schools to avoid these issues.

We agreed to disagree, but it's worth noting that criminalizing perceptions and victim-blaming of Black and Brown girls is also a pattern in private and parochial schools, as it is in charter and traditional public schools.[20] Even wealthy, high-performing districts have documented racial disparities along these lines.

At the conclusion of the meeting, a white officer walked up to me and asked, "You really don't believe that kids who are causing trouble should stay in schools, do you?"

"If you work in a school, you should believe in the promise of all children," I repeated.

"Yeah, but some kids may need to be removed," he said.

"But we can't start there. Or leave them there. Our goal has to be to reconnect them with schools. There's a reason they're being disruptive. That's what we have to figure out," I said.

The officer nodded in agreement.

A different African American officer who had been listening nearby chimed in quietly. "You know, I know what you're saying," he said to me. "Some of us are trying to make sure these kids stay connected."

He handed me his *alternative* business card, the one associated with a community-based organization that provides tutoring and mentorship to students. Their goal is to foster relationships that can support positive life outcomes for high-need students. I appreciated the exchange because it signaled that he understood what I hope we all will come to understand—that relationships and being in community are healing. Everything else, all the actions that do not heal, are Band-Aids at best and scarlet letters of at worst. Isolation—facilitated by exclusionary discipline and arrest—simply reinforces the conditions that are at the root of student conflict.

In *Killing the Black Body*, Dorothy Roberts described a jarring episode in this nation's history of pathologizing Black children. In many cases, this sort of framing begins with the circumstances of birth. She wrote:

> Many Americans believe not only that Black mothers are likely to corrupt their children, but that Black children are predisposed to corruption. . . . It was erroneously reported that these children sustained neurological injuries that warped their emotional development, making them unresponsive as babies and uncontrollable as toddlers. Newspaper stories warned of a horde of Black children about to descend on inner-city kindergartens in need of high-cost special services. But the brain damage crack babies sustained was supposed to cut even deeper: lacking in innate social conscience, crack babies were destined to grow up to be criminals.[21]

Just as these aspersive narratives about Black children as "animals" predestined to become criminals were being presented to the public, there was a steady rollback of integration efforts. Our schools became less integrated and increasingly extensions of the carceral state. For girls of color in K–12 schools, like their counterparts in actual lockups, this meant that their well-being depended on censoring their verbal and nonverbal expressions. Their attitudes were subjected to as much scrutiny and regulation as their behaviors. This is why Black girls and other girls of color have been among the leading voices that challenge our political reflex to increase surveillance and policing in schools. Running schools as detention centers means that the harmful triggers that typically exist for girls in punitive institutions are now present for them in places that should be safe, nurturing learning environments.

⌒

On February 13, 2018, seventeen students and faculty members were killed by a nineteen-year-old gunman at Marjory Stoneman Douglas High School in Parkland, Florida. The nation was horrified and shocked by the actions of a student who trained with white nationalists to unleash terror upon his former school community. A swell of advocacy for gun-control laws and for revision of school safety practices inundated local and national news outlets.

"I want to be a part of Stoneman Douglas and I want to live out the rest of my high school career normally. But there's no such thing as normal anymore," Samantha Fuentes, a high school senior healing from a bullet wound to the thigh, told CNN.[22]

Much of the public dialogue about the incident—particularly from the students—was restricted by fear. Without a full inclusion of the voices of students of color, particularly Black students, the national public policy discussion centered primarily on ways to *increase* the presence of guns on campus, rather than reduce it.

Donald Trump proposed to arm one-fifth of all teachers and hire military veterans as security guards. "A teacher would have a concealed gun on them. They'd go for special training and they would be there and you would no longer be a gun-free zone," Trump reportedly said. "You'd have a lot of people that would be armed, that'd be ready."[23]

The president's recommendation reflected a growing sentiment in the public that conflates safety in schools with the presence of armed adults—a militarized school environment run more like a police state than a space for learning, growth, and development. Missing, however, was input from Black students (11 percent of the school's student population), who had expressed concerns about the call to increase police presence and armed surveillance on campus.

"Black and Brown men and women are disproportionately targeted and killed by law enforcement . . . these are not facts I can live with comfortably," said Tyah-Amoy Roberts in a student-led press conference on the matter.[24]

For these students, like many others throughout the nation, police presence in schools *reinforces* the threat of violence. Prior to this incident, I spoke with girls in Nashville, Tennessee, about the issue of policing in schools.

"I see more police officers in Black schools," one of the girls said.

"When you see a police officer, you're not thinking 'He's here to protect me,'" said another girl. "We've seen Trayvon Martin and Rodney King and . . ."

Surveillance is not safety; neither is intimidation and threat.

"We don't need police," said another girl in the room. "We need a sense of community."

⌒

There is no question that our students have experienced—and inherited—enough violence. Young people protesting gun violence from private citizens is like young people protesting state violence. The instinct to stay alive is the same, and the stress caused by the threat of violence from any source impedes their ability to learn.

Historically, the political reflex in this country has been violent. Policy makers have responded to youth efforts to *curb* their exposure to violence, quite astoundingly, with calls to *further* militarize our nation's schools and communities—to increase armed security, install bulletproof windows, and even to arm teachers. This is what we offer students, despite plenty of research and evidence that prevention of trauma and responses to it should revolve around trained counselors and grief specialists, for the direct and vicarious trauma that students experience after being exposed to violence is an assault on their lives and humanity.[25]

The racial isolation produced by narratives about "dangerous" students of color has allowed the justification of increasingly punitive responses to adolescent behavior. It has led to a failure to recognize and respond to the trauma of trying to grow up in a society predisposed to a racism that thrives on the social, physical, intellectual, and spiritual exploitation and underdevelopment of Black and Brown youth. Police patrolling of hallways is a symbolic gesture of intimidation, and it reinforces the idea that our children are inherently in need of police interventions, rather than the interventions of skilled youth specialists, mentors, nutritionists, and therapists. These are expectations we set up, and they have become the groundwork for our pedagogical approach to school safety and discipline. When the police presence in a school is significant, it signals that our institutions have accepted a belief that our children are predisposed to criminal behavior. *That* is the intention—stated or otherwise—set for our students by the places charged with helping them flourish.

For our girls especially, we must continue to interrogate how this framework casts their development as deviant—as cell bound—and how this priming can reduce their capacity to be scholars and diminish the overall well-being of their communities.

Our positive intentions are sometimes obscured by our actions and the infrastructure we build, defend, and maintain. Our challenge is to set a different intention for our children.

Foundations for Transformation

In 2017, Canada's largest school district, Toronto District Schools, voted to remove school resource officers from schools.[26] The result of community organizing and the school board responding to the voices of those most marginalized by the presence of police in schools, Toronto demonstrated that alternatives to a culture of surveillance are possible.

With intention, many schools are realizing that safety is not a function of external inputs—police, for example—but rather is about building relationships with students that foster trust and accountability. A pedagogy by which girls of color learn in spaces absent a criminalizing infrastructure requires revising our assumptions about harm and safety and about the conditions at the core of their oppression. According to DePaul University's Stephen Nathan Haymes, "a pedagogy of Black urban struggle linked to a representational pedagogy would recognize that Black self-contempt is the result of Blacks . . . using white supremacist definitions of race and Blackness. . . . Mainstream white consumer culture [is what] a pedagogy of place for Black urban struggle must critically interrogate in terms of its influences on the formation of Black identity and Black public space."[27]

The new urban struggle, in this case, is to interrogate conditions that reflect white supremacist understandings of Black and Brown identities, as well as conditions that produce policies and practices that result in their criminalization. We can begin by asking questions about how the assumption of criminality influences the environments we create for girls of color and other students in schools. These questions might include:

- When are law enforcement officers called to intervene? Is this written in a Memorandum of Understanding?
- What *continuum of interventions* exists, or could we create, to respond to conflict among students, or between students and adults, that does not include the intervention of a law enforcement officer?
- What training do educators and school leaders need in order to more effectively respond to conflict in schools *without* calling the police?
- When law enforcement officers are called in to respond to legitimate threats to safety, are they trained to be culturally competent and trauma responsive in schools?

A critical interrogation of instruments of surveillance should provide new spaces for learning that are free from the norms built by the tools of oppression. According to Western notions of freedom, "policing" is a necessary function in society to maintain social order. However, rather than focusing on maintaining

social order and presuming criminality from the outset, real
safety grows out of facilitating the conditions of freedom, healing, and relationship building. Relying on forces specifically
designed to control behavior and be the first point of contact
with the criminal legal system is not intended to result in a
culture of healing—and it never will. But a culture of healing
is essential for combating and reducing violence and trauma in
our schools.

To support a new pedagogy on school safety, we must establish
and expand our understanding of what it means to feel *safe*. This
begins with an unequivocal rejection of the dehumanization
of girls of color. How are girls defining safety for themselves?
Referring to students—even the ones who get into trouble—as
"juvenile delinquents," "troublemakers," "offenders" or other
nomenclature associated with the court and criminal legal system normalizes the expectation of their involvement with systems that we don't want raising or educating our children. It
primes them for underperformance and stifles their capacity
to awaken a sense of belonging and development in school. Put
simply, we can ask, do we want girls to end up in criminal systems? No. So let's engage them accordingly.

There are other options.

⌒

"Take off your hat," a commanding, elderly voice said from
behind me.

I was visiting an alternative public school in San Diego, California, that was tasked with educating high school students
returning to the community after incarceration. Many of the

students were described as "rowdy" by the educators around them, but they appeared to behave like other teens their age— being a little flirtatious with their peers, or raising their voices in the hallway between classes.

I was walking with the principal of the school. He was showing me around and describing the various programs he had put in place for his female students, who were disproportionately Black and Latinx. But then I heard the voice, so I turned around. Whoever made the request meant business.

I was not wearing a hat, so I assumed the voice was talking to a student. I turned to see a tall young man walking down a corridor of the school slightly behind a group of students. Beside him was a smaller Black woman, who continued to tell him that he needed to get to class. He looked at her, she looked back . . . and then he removed his hat and walked to class. I guessed her age at around seventy.

"Who was that?" I asked the principal.

"Oh, she's one of our grandmothers," he said with a smile. "Everybody knows not to mess with the grandmothers."

I gasped, then laughed. It was brilliant! There were no police patrolling the hallways. Instead, there were groups of elderly women, lovingly referred to as "the grandmothers," who walked students between classes and helped to maintain order in the classroom. The principal had built a school infrastructure that was less criminalizing of students who had already been down that road, so that they could feel a sense of community, comfort, and safety. With less confrontation, there was less fighting, according to this principal, which provided space for love to work its magic. For girls and other students who were parenting, the presence of the grandmothers provided additional support besides the day-care on campus, filling an important space for young people longing for the loving attention of adults.

Cultivating safe spaces for girls of color in the learning environment includes more than simply removing law enforcement and other instruments of surveillance from schools. My conversations with girls of color throughout the country reveal that they feel safer in schools that have cultivated spaces for them to learn without the stress of racism, sexism, racialized sexism, Islamophobia, homophobia, transphobia, ableism, and other biases that marginalize students, who are culturally and linguistically diverse.

Schools that *theorize* and *practice* safety as a function of trust and love—rather than a function of surveillance or the threat of arrest or removal from school—can produce higher-achieving students and achieve robust inclusion of students who might otherwise be cast out to the margins. As students' brains process this safety, their defense mechanisms relax and they are more able to counter the narratives of dehumanization that have come to define them. Their lives become narratives that defy the justification for police in schools in the first place. Their blues become songs of praise.

Interlude

"Are We Actually Trying to Be Here for Young People?"

There was a recent incident in South Carolina where the classmate of a Black girl drew a picture of the KKK hanging someone.

He was a white boy and handed it to the Black girl, and said, "This is for you."

She told the teacher what happened, and said, "He's being racist. He's actually threatening me. What do we do?"

The teacher said, "That's a stretch. Go have a seat."

The Black girl gets dismissed from class, goes to the assistant principal and the principal, and they're like, "We'll handle it."

But let's look at how they handled it.

The white boy who drew the picture—his mother was called in to get him. They sent the Black girl back to class. There was no parent called to say, "Come comfort your child because she's totally upset." She was sent back to class. And then, as the day went on, they're like, "Okay, he's going to be expelled . . . he's never coming back to school again."

The Black girl is walking down the hall, and who does she run into? The boy and his family. He wasn't expelled.

The SRO who they called in later—maybe two or three days later, to investigate—said, "We don't see any wrongdoing." Yet the school still suspended him because he threatened the life of a child.

And the police were like, "Oh, we think it's just boys being boys."

The girl is going to school . . . she says, "I love school. I want to be a veterinarian. I have so many dreams, but I don't know . . . I just don't think it's possible anymore. I don't have a thrill for anything."

So when we meet with the principal, he's like, "Yeah, I should have told you, . . . but we can't put the toothpaste back in the tube, so where do we move from here?"

We're talking about a girl with a 3.6 GPA. You know what they told her? "We're so glad you didn't get loud or try to hurt him, because we would have had to arrest you."

There was no comfort.

Six weeks later, she's up in the middle of the night. She's scared.

She said, "I just feel that y'all don't care about me."

The principal was like, "We're going to send you to the school psychologist."

Six weeks later! Why wasn't that one of the first things? Why didn't the school psychologist and social worker step up and say, "This is what we need to be interacting with?"

The school found all of the social and emotional support for *him*. They looked at this girl—who was five-feet, six inches tall and about two hundred pounds, and they said, "You're okay. Go back to class."

When we talk about these things, we can talk about SROs, but the teacher who didn't respond when we first went there, the assistant principal who sent her back to her classroom, the social worker—all these people who didn't respond to this Black girl . . . I think it's a larger conversation when we start talking about safety and what Black girls deserve, and what girls of color deserve.

We're still saying, "These girls don't fit into the mold." We're supposed to be so beyond race. But we have to work with adults around the trauma that they're carrying that they pass down to our young people.

Hurt people, hurt people—I see them in the school system, where they show up most. Adults can show so much power because we see our children as "less than," versus saying, "these are the people who are going to be making all of the decisions for us, so it's our responsibility to build them up."

I get so emotional. . . . Why do we criminalize kids for the harm that adults do? And then we want them to be accountable to make our stuff okay? We've got to check ourselves! Are we just about policing, or are we actually trying to be here for young people?

Vivian Anderson
EveryBlackGirl, Inc.
South Carolina

Track 4
Nobody Knows My Name

Mapping the Margins for Our Most Vulnerable Girls

Nobody knows my name.
Nobody knows what I've done.

. . .

I ain't no high yella.
I'm a deep killer brown.
I ain't gonna marry,
Ain't gonna settle down.
I'm gonna drink good moonshine . . .
See that long lonesome road?

—Bessie Smith, "Young Woman's Blues"
(Columbia, 1926)

In late 2017, I was asked to testify before the U.S. Commission on Civil Rights about the racial disparities affecting school

discipline among girls of color with disabilities. Approximately
6.5 million students nationwide receive special education, and
90 percent of those students have high-incidence disabilities,
described as "specific learning disabilities, speech or language
impairments, other health impairments, autism, intellectual
disabilities, and emotional disturbance."[1] Disabilities may also
include hearing loss, poor vision or blindness, impaired mobil-
ity, or less visible disabilities, such as chronic pain disorder or
epilepsy.* Black girls with disabilities are two or three times as
likely as their white counterparts to be suspended or arrested.[2]

Though uncertain about the extent to which people would
be prepared to discuss the unique ways in which girls of color,
particularly African American girls with disabilities, experience school discipline, I stepped into the briefing ready to share
analyses from the National Black Women's Justice Institute.
The research we had done found that, while students with disabilities were more vulnerable than those without to experience discipline in schools, racial disparities were also prevalent,
particularly among girls.[3] As I approached the room filled with
commissioners and the public, I wondered how many had ever
been educators—or how many would have spent time with students with disabilities, let alone those who had experienced rou-

---

* Disabilities range widely in type and presentation and may also include
learning disabilities, such as attention-deficit hyperactivity disorder, dys-
lexia, or dyscalculia; chronic health disorders, such as epilepsy, Crohn's
disease, arthritis, cancer, diabetes, migraine headaches, or multiple scle-
rosis; psychological or psychiatric disabilities, such as mood, anxiety and
depressive disorders, or post-traumatic stress disorder (PTSD); traumatic
brain injury; etc. See "Teaching Students with Disabilities," Vanderbilt
University Center for Teaching, https://cft.vanderbilt.edu/guides-sub
-pages/disabilities.

tine school-based discipline or criminalization associated with their condition. I wondered even more how many had interacted regularly with girls of color within these conditions. I expected to occupy a unique voice in the discussion. So I came prepared to show that the statistics reveal a narrative of exclusion—Black and Latinx girls with disabilities being removed from school and criminalized via suspension, referral to law enforcement, and arrest at disproportionately high rates.

This was my downbeat. My blues. My truth.

I wanted to elevate the importance of these disparities, because they signal the potential presence of differential treatment. Black girls with disabilities are the most likely among girls to be removed from school or be in contact with the juvenile court system as a result of behaviors deemed problematic or negative. Yet they are *under*represented among girls who are offered appropriate interventions that repair harm and relationships so as to reestablish their identities as learners. We all had to believe that this situation was dire.

Suddenly I realized that, along with legal scholar and researcher Daniel Losen, I had spent the better part of an hour trying to establish that the pattern of differential treatment was even worthy of the commission's action. Disagreements about whether schools could be biased because they were institutions (and not people) seemed to me to occupy too much time, especially because it's *people* who build and maintain institutions. While researchers were parsing numbers, arguing about statistical significance and methodology, I kept thinking of the real children who bear the impact of institutional failures to respond to their needs. In my mind popped the face of a Latinx high school student, who—bound to a wheelchair—came up to me after a lecture just to thank me for doing the bare minimum of "talk-ing about girls like me." She was just happy to be included. Yet the issue of worthiness, of justifying the mere discussion, was dominating the hearing. This was too low a bar for a conversa-tion about equity and education.

In our commitment to prove how much we *know*, sometimes we forget to focus on how much we don't appear to care. This is what was on my mind when I signaled that I wanted to make a statement:

> I think it's important for us to elevate in this conver-sation how oppression manifests. Oppression mani-fests structurally, individually, culturally, and in internalized ways. Knowing that, we cannot say that schools, as institutions, cannot be biased. Structured decision-making tools to help educators respond to the specific needs of students do help to improve the outcomes. They help teachers respond to conflicts on campus and incidents of trauma, to engage their capacity to ask questions in ways that will be respon-sive to children.

I had hoped that we could acknowledge that Black and Brown children's disabilities are underdiagnosed in many areas (includ-ing hearing and vision), and overdiagnosed for emotional issues.[4] Not only does the absence of diagnoses prevent treat-ment and appropriate institutional response, but also the bias-es that inform interactions with these students foster a lack of patience among adults, who then respond to negative behaviors with punishment rather than care.

"I am personally less interested in how we parse numbers to see if students are being disproportionately harmed than I am in ways to ensure that *all* students are receiving equitable treatment. *One* student is too many. And if *one* student is too many, then we have to do something differently. If one classroom is not functioning with competence and engagement, without racial, gender, and disability bias, then we're not doing enough."

It wasn't that I was not interested in establishing disparity and investigating whether there is a pattern of discrimination. That was obviously important. It was the implicit suggestion that if the numbers don't provide a "statistically significant" argument for pain, then it doesn't exist. Numbers never tell the whole story. That was and is the problem. Every child affected by injustice is worthy of our attention, but each child may or may not show up as a statistic.

In conclusion, I said, "The extent to which we can develop tools, guidance, training, technical assistance, and rigorous engagement of participatory methods so as to include those who are impacted by these conditions in the conversation *about* these conditions is all-important to our development of a capacity to be as responsive as we can."

After listening to my testimony and that of the other panelists, Commissioner Peter Kirsanow stated, "This has been very stimulating and informative, and I appreciate all the hard work all of you put into it. Our charter's view on civil rights is to investigate and analyze disparities based on discrimination, based on *discrimination*, based on protected classes such as race, disability. We are not a commission of best educational practices."

This is where policy makers responsible for upholding equity in policy, even if well-intentioned, get it wrong. It *is* our collective, ongoing job to seek *best educational practice*, because it is central to ensuring the absence of discrimination, particularly for the students who are most marginalized by status quo policies and practices.

Again, it was my downbeat. My blues. My truth. And I knew it to be the truth of other educators and educational advocates who love racially, culturally, and linguistically diverse students, with and without disabilities, and who want policies that support their capacity to practice better pedagogical approaches and enact policies to help students rather than criminalize them.

My written testimony included a number of specific recommendations to address the differential discipline of Black girls and other students with disabilities. Among them was a call for the U.S. Department of Education, which had taken steps toward rescinding discipline guidelines and other protections for disabled students,[5] to maintain federal guidance on these matters. I also recommended that additional legislative efforts be instituted at the federal, state, and local levels to limit schools' ability to arbitrarily shorten the learning day for students with disabilities and to improve their documentation and monitoring of informal removals from school that do not result in suspensions or expulsions.

I recommended that districtwide policies include a robust articulation of gender equity and student-focused response to sexual assault, including specific supports for survivors with disabilities. Black girls with disabilities are uniquely vulnerable to sexual assault in schools, as in other public and private spaces. Disabled girls like Sandra have written this truth:

> Being disabled, considered high functioning, and a girl is a very unique intersection. The rapid development of my body skewed my treatment as well. I was hyper-sexualized because of my body and fetishized on the presumption that my neurotype prohibited me from knowing what sex entails. . . . 83% of disabled women will be sexually assaulted in their lifetime. 60% of black girls have been sexually assaulted before reaching the age of 18, and when you intersect those two marginalizations, the chance of that child coming of age without being assaulted is slim to none.[6]

Girls with and without disabilities need to feel safe from sexual violence and harassment in schools. Protection from sexual assault is a human and civil right that requires accountability and enforcement from the community and sometimes the legal system, particularly through prevention programs and responsive services associated with the Department of Justice Office on Violence Against Women, but also through consistent monitoring and coordinated response. The National Women's Law Center has offered several suggestions for ensuring that a school's sexual harassment policy is effective, including:

- Clear and well-publicized policies and procedures
- A clear definition of sexual harassment and possible disciplinary actions

- Involvement of the entire school community to make the policy "user-friendly"
- Confidentiality
- Safeguards against retaliation
- A clear explanation of how students facing harassment can challenge it, including how, when, and with whom a complaint can be filed.[7]

Educators should act immediately when confronted with sexual harassment. Across the country, girls of color report that when they experience inappropriate touching, grabbing, pointing, suggestive looks and stares, and other forms of harassment, educators either turn their heads or suggest that these are no big deal. But girls who feel they are unsafe are more likely to avoid school, fight, or engage in hostile behavior as a protective action against such assaults.

The U.S. Department of Education under the leadership of Betsy DeVos has become increasingly less sympathetic to the voices of survivors, undermining the "me too" movement, which has sought to publicize the prevalence of sexual violence, and other efforts among survivors, advocates, and scholars who have been working to end gender-based violence. For Black and Brown girls, this federal neglect can have grave implications. For girls who are already less likely to be believed, guidance from a federal agency that places additional barriers before her as she seeks healing, reconciliation, and accountability can make coming forward even less likely. Of course, federal guidance is helpful, but we have to understand that the liberation of these girls—and the safety they seek in schools—is not something they can rely on the federal government to provide. Their well-being is too important to be left to the whims of politicians.

For survivors, healing may operate on half time while the work around them functions at double time. Stated differently, healing takes time, and they need the freedom and safety to honor their process in accord with the best practices associated with responding to trauma. Survivors also need a political climate that recognizes their vulnerability. Then the institutional processes can more effectively respond to them—and to the persons who have caused them harm. This process is local and should involve people affected at the local level.

For example, California's Bay Area Alliance for Girls developed a student-driven policy platform to stop sexual harassment in schools, which includes prioritizing the survivor's emotional and psychological health, ensuring that survivor voices are included in the resolution of the complaint, and that restorative approaches are considered in the repair of harm. According to sujatha baliga, director of the Restorative Justice Project at Impact Justice, schools that use restorative approaches to sexual violence on campus have produced transformative results, wherein the young people involved experience a greater satisfaction with the process and fuller recovery from the harm.

On this matter, sujatha—who has facilitated restorative circles in response to sexual violence with high school students—has pointed out that a study in California of a countywide effort found that "youth who participated in the program were 44 percent less likely to commit future crimes than those whose crimes were addressed through the county's juvenile justice system."[8] School districts with platforms that reflect an intersectional analysis of equity and include trauma- and healing-informed strategies to uplift the protection of students' rights to learn in harassment-free environments are *safer*.

Responding to the Whole Person

Girls of color who experience substance use disorder and dependency or incarceration, or who express their gender or sexuality along a continuum or in nonbinary ways are uniquely vulnerable to marginalization in the learning space. Bias against them and their lived experiences is often coded in language, policies, and practices that undermine their capacity to fully recognize their potential as scholars.

Black and Brown girls who express their gender identity and sexuality along a continuum can be invisible in discussions, practices, and policies that seek to improve educational conditions for youth. To be clear, one's sexual and gender identity does not necessarily place one out on the margins. However, to reach those who are at greatest risk of harm, we cannot shape our understanding of an issue only from the experiences of those who have resources or connections. Many girls of color who also identify as Lesbian, Gay, Bisexual, Pansexual, Queer or Questioning, and/or may identify as Trans and/or Nonbinary, are among some of the most marginalized in our learning spaces. A study by Girls for Gender Equity, in which 53 percent of participants were Black, 23 percent were Latinx, and nearly 7 percent were Gender Queer or Trans and Gender Non-Conforming (TGNC), found that in New York City, "girls and TGNC youth of color experience institutional violence in schools" and "interpersonal violence in school from adults and their peers."[9] Together these identities can make some of our young people the most vulnerable to high ACEs scores and exclusionary discipline, putting them on track to experience contact with the juvenile court and/or criminal legal system.

A bias-free environment for students of color who identify as LGB and TGNC removes their burden of having to "decide every day between attending school in a hostile climate and the possibility of experiencing harassment or skipping school and the possibility of facing punitive discipline measures for absence and even truancy charges."[10] In Miami, during a panel discussion on biases facing Black girls and nonbinary youth, young activist Mason captured it by stating, "We're told 'You're not your body,' until you say your body doesn't match you. . . . Then you're *only* your body." Providing supportive resources with a commitment to accepting and being in alliance with LGB and TGNC students helps to generate a culture of inclusion that goes beyond "bare minimum" efforts, such as gender-neutral bathroom options and signage that articulates the LGBTQ-friendliness of a school.[11]

A 2019 report by the National Black Women's Justice Institute written by researcher Andrea Ritchie, offers a call for the expansion of the framework by which educators, and others in communities that work with youth, can become better allies in supporting their safety. In the report, Ritchie writes, "Criminal responses to sexual violence often don't increase safety for Black women, girls, trans, gender nonconforming and nonbinary people and often leave them unprotected, unbelieved, and without agency or a long-term remedy for root causes of the violence and exploitation they have experienced."[12] As such, among the recommendations to better respond to the sexual violence affecting these populations of youth is the call for the creation of "mechanisms for students, parents, teachers, and counselors to co-create transformative approaches to school safety."[13]

As noted earlier, girls who experience substance use disorder or incarceration are also among the most vulnerable to exclusionary discipline. They should also be able to find spaces to address their trauma, to avoid the stigmatization and labeling that too often spreads among their peers—and educators, too, as they seek to build an educational journey that can create opportunities for them. Many of the teenage girls whom I have had an opportunity to engage describe their schools as particularly ill-equipped to respond to them when they were in moments of crisis associated with substance use or contact with the juvenile court. This is something every school must reconcile to become a location for healing.

According to the National Institute on Drug Abuse, there are thirteen principles of adolescent substance use disorder treatment:

1. Adolescent substance use needs to be identified and addressed as soon as possible.
2. Adolescents can benefit from a drug abuse intervention even if they are not diagnosed with a disorder.
3. Routine medical visits each year are an opportunity to talk to teens about drug abuse.
4. Legal interventions and sanctions or family pressure may play an important role in getting adolescents to enter and stay in treatment.

5. Substance use disorder treatment should be tailored to the unique needs of the adolescent, based upon an assessment of strengths, weaknesses, school performance, cultural and ethnic factors, and special physical or behavioral issues, among others.

6. Treatment should address the needs of the whole person, not just her drug abuse.

7. Behavioral therapies are effective in addressing adolescent drug abuse.

8. Families and community are important aspects of treatment.

9. Effectively treating substance use disorders in adolescents requires us to identify and treat other mental health conditions.

10. Sensitive issues, such as violence and child abuse or risk of suicide, should be identified and addressed.

11. If relapse occurs, it is important to monitor drug use during treatment.

12. Staying in treatment for an "adequate period of time" (three months or more) and continuity of care are important.

13. Treating adolescents for sexually transmitted diseases is an important part of treatment.[14]

These are all important considerations for educators to be aware of—even if some of them feel disconnected to practices in the classroom or school community. The school can be a primary trigger for girls grappling with substance use disorder.

For example, Tee, a survivor of commercial sex trafficking, once described her public high school as a place where she could reliably buy marijuana easily. She recognized early on that her high school was a location for many of her triggers—specifically sex and drugs.

"What could they do?" she asked me one day. "I mean, kids shouldn't be able to buy drugs at school, but I'm not sure there's more they could do for me."

The truth is, if the school had been openly addressing these principles or forging partnerships to help students understand drug use as a public health issue (as opposed to a criminal issue), there is a lot that could have been done, such as developing youth-led educational and skills training programs. Effective school-based interventions among teens and adolescents show that while there are multiple levels of influence that can contribute to substance use disorder (e.g., knowledge of risks associated with use, experiencing harsh discipline, poor parental monitoring, lack of relationship with teachers, low engagement with school, among others), schools should use peer education, media and public policy analysis to address the issue.[15] Put it out there. Speak on the issue as blues women did. By not discussing substance use or simply removing students from campus without building community in other ways, they were actually keeping the subculture alive, and thus girls like Tee unsafe.

Intersectionality is a useful theoretical tool by which to develop responses to girls of color who have been marginalized from schools. It is a framework that considers how identities intersect to inform experiences with institutions, individuals, and systems. Educational institutions, practitioners, and policy makers must shift their collective worldview if they are to realize their capacity to reach girls of color who have been most marginalized in their learning spaces or related conditions. Instead of immediately responding to children as "problematic," probe what's at the root of negative behavior. Instead of waiting until something goes wrong at school, establish relationships with students early. Research by Professor Ronald Dahl and his collaborators shows that adolescents are not "passive learners conforming to adult values," and that young people experience "a greater sensitivity to interventions at this stage in life."[16] This means girls vulnerable to conflict in school should not be cast away as "lost causes." Invest in them. Actively *care* about them.

Overall, educators can reduce discrimination by acting as facilitators of best educational practice. An inclusive, participatory pedagogy facilitates healing because a comprehensive commitment to address biases—particularly against those furthest on the margins—rejects structures of oppression. Structures of oppression are dismantled through participatory learning and practices that engage and respond to the source of our collective disharmony: fear.

Centering the most marginalized among our girls of color allows for a critical discourse about the skills required to meet these girls where they are, and about what we can do to guide them toward the realization of their full potential. Whereas other pedagogical models emphasize learning about home conditions or lived experiences to teach, or focusing on questioning to facilitate learning, a liberative pedagogy for Black and Brown girls is driven by opportunities for these girls to co-create the content and conditions of their learning. Helping girls develop what bell hooks called an "oppositional gaze" is a critical way to begin this level of involvement. This activates what Black feminist scholars call a "critical feminist media pedagogy," by exploring gender notes, beliefs, identities, and socializations. According to education scholar Charlotte Jacobs:

> Instead of serving as sites of reproduction of negative messages and images concerning Black girls, schools can potentially transform into spaces where Black girls are given the tools to recognize, critique, and push back narratives that oppress and dominate Black girls and women, particularly those messages found in the media.[17]

To be free of criminalization, they need a place to be the leaders, to repurpose their pain, and to apply the lessons they learn in life to the theories and concepts they learn in the classroom. They need school to be a place where they can tap into the source of their healing.

This is the critical lesson before living.

The EMERGE pilot educational reentry program has taken this very approach to working with girls who have experienced learning (and sometimes life) against some of significant obstacles. The program is designed to interrupt school-to-confinement pathways for girls who have struggled in traditional (or even alternative) schools. Girls in the program are typically ages sixteen to eighteen, have had a severe interruption in their learning trajectory (expulsion, truancy, etc.), and may have been in contact with the child welfare and/or criminal legal system. A number of girls in the program have been commercially sexually exploited. In fact, there are students in the program with ACEs scores as high as nine. In other words, the girls and young women in this program understand the margins quite well.

As a partner in the creation of this program and the lead internal evaluator, I went to visit our first cohort of girls to explain how our evaluation was going to work. Typically, a participatory project engages the impacted group in a cyclical process of planning, action, observation, and reflection.[18] The girls were busy working in the classroom but seemed genuinely interested in how their experiences might shape the development of the pilot project's work with them, and how the district might understand "what works" in educating girls of color with similar experiences.

"So . . . we're research?" one of the girls asked.

"Yes," I said. "But you're also the *researchers.*"

She nodded and smiled.

Participatory processes are central to the healing methods of blues women. They know what they know, and they know *that* they know it. Engaging models that provide space to develop reasoning skills and the opportunity to build from their multiple ways of knowing—extended epistemology—gives girls a chance to center their experiences, tell stories, dance, sing, write, meditate, and play their knowledge into a curriculum that recognizes and values these expressions as commensurate with the other "data" they will learn in school. Action-oriented processes that involve narrative inquiry, appreciative inquiry, cooperative inquiry, and other modes of participatory research have been used in educational settings as a way to not only increase the capacity of the student journey to be at its best, but also to help the school function as a more efficient institution.* This type of transformational planning process opens the realm of possibility beyond what we think is probable, and moves us to explore what is *possible*. That's the magical zone where girls furthest on the margins often find themselves.

We teach our children that "sharing is caring." However, we treat knowledge and the distribution of good ideas as commodities. This inconsistency does a disservice to girls who are involved in multiple systems, whose identities are rendered invisible and/or mischaracterized, and who are in the best position to collectively plan and act toward their own freedom. The work of EMERGE continues to be workshopped, refined, and developed, but there is a collection of valuable observations about promising strategies that educators may consider when co-constructing learning environments for our most marginalized girls. First, instead of approaching the classroom as a traditional learning space, educators might allot time for the girls to share their feelings, hesitations, and initial thoughts coming into the classroom. Being consistent in the approach and delivery of messages, and creating an in-class routine helps to facilitate comfort in the room. Check-ins at the start of class and breathing

---

* Participatory action research is a family of action-oriented research methods that include narrative inquiry, appreciative inquiry, and cooperative inquiry. Narrative inquiry is the centering of one's narrative, or life story, as a way of knowing in participatory research. Appreciative inquiry centers the unconditional positive question in the collection and interpretation of data in participatory science. Cooperative inquiry is a cyclical process for understanding through personal inquiry. See Peter Reason and Hilary Bradbury, *The Sage Handbook of Action Research: Participative Inquiry and Practice* (Los Angeles: Sage Publications, 2008).

exercises or quiet time to write in a journal or on a shared topic are effective strategies to bring girls into a positive mental space. Providing time to shape and process their thoughts is important. Second, relevant instructor training (e.g., bias removal, culturally responsive instruction, restorative justice, integrated learning, etc.) is essential to preparing educators for this work.

It is not easy to interact with highly traumatized or marginalized girls, which is why aligning actions with the set intentions is paramount. It is critical for the lead instructor to have specific experience in working with young people who have experienced multiple forms of trauma and who have been involved with multiple legal and social systems. Experience is one way that we *know*. It can be emotionally dangerous for everyone when educators or staff with little or no experience in trauma-informed work end up engaging girls who are survivors, without close supervision.

To appropriately respond to the educational needs of girls of color who are in contact with the juvenile legal system and those who are routinely exposed to exclusionary discipline, it is imperative to work in small groups and engage in rigorous, culturally responsive teaching practices.[19] Meaningful relationships with the students create learning environments that are flexible, open, and responsive to the needs of girls on these margins. It is also important to note that the healing-informed approach to education and instruction helps girls overcome many of their concerns regarding their ability to share space with girls with whom they've had conflict.

Early observations and discussions with girls involved with multiple systems have revealed that they're often involved with these systems because of their childhood trauma. The last thing we want schools to do is reinforce the harm they already experience elsewhere. Part of the process of being healing-responsive is to center the appreciative, positive condition in their lives and provide opportunity for them to articulate and realize their own goals. Rebuilding relationships with school and interrupting school-to-confinement pathways requires the ability to respond to the individual needs of the students in an effort to keep their risk of confinement from escalating. A critical component of working with survivors of violence and victimization is to understand the depth and complexity of the challenges they face. Too often they face homelessness, rejection, criminalization, abuse, and exploitation. Individually and collectively, these traumatic life experiences affect the way in which girls traverse thresholds to the world around them. This is not work for a single person. It really does take a village.

Foundations for Transformation

Several interventions have emerged as promising among some of our schools' most marginalized girls:

- **Weekly discussion groups** that engage girls in Black feminist theory, intersectionality, and "street fiction," give teachers the opportunity to "develop a rapport with the girls so that their space [feels] supportive and inclusive of all who attend."[20]
- **Critical media literacy** (including online) aids students to "clarify the world around them—helping them see how society functions and make their own decisions about how they choose to represent" themselves, and that provides

them with an opportunity to situate their lives in the context of constructed norms around them.[21]

• **Culturally responsive programming to promote sisterhood** gives everyone a chance to map a reduction in aggressive behavior and fighting. One study found that teachers observed noticeable differences in the behavior of Black girls who participated in an intervention based on the principles of Kwanzaa, noting that "on days when the students received the intervention their behavior significantly improved."[22]

• **Black girlhood studies** is what Dominique Hill calls a "mattering project," meaning it centers the experiences of these girls as essential knowing. Similarly, Vera López and Meda Chesney-Lind find that Latinx girls' perceptions of themselves often challenge pervasive stereotypes about their identities, paving a way toward Latina girlhood studies.[23] These efforts intentionally and specifically address the erasure issue that Black and Brown girls note as an insult to their identities as scholars.[24] Related to this is the development of Black girls' competencies in imaginative literature. In *Even Cinderella Is White: (Re)Centering Black Girls' Voices as Literacies of Resistance*, educators Jeremiah Young, Marquita Foster, and Dorothy Hines propose "counter fairytales," an activity that "encourages girls to take traditional fairy tales and rewrite the narrative from their perspective," letting them envision themselves as "queens and princesses."[25]

For those among our students who identify as nonbinary or for whom princess narratives are undesirable, reading urban fiction is another way to "deconstruct and challenge stereotyping and dominant messages" about Black and Brown experiences. These "super-girl" narratives often uplift the development of counternarratives that challenge structures and stories of racialized gender bias in the United States.[26]

Educators working with high-risk girls must understand that adults cannot empower youth, but they can give girls the tools to be and feel empowered. At the center of the effort to improve their educational outcomes must be an emphasis on students' personal development. Educators must prioritize creating opportunities for girls to create organic and supportive networks among themselves. When this happens, girls with problematic educational histories begin to consider the school *their* school, as opposed to just the school that they *attend*.

⌒

"I'm done!" one of the EMERGE girls declared. "Can I just draw a picture or something?"

She was exasperated and visibly exhausted—partially from spending several hours working on a science assignment. She pushed a stack of papers away from her and toward Randa, the program director. Randa first looked at her tentatively, and then reached out to collect the packet of materials.

"Did you finish the packet?" Randa asked.

"No," the girl said. "I'm done. It's my sister's birthday and I want to make her a poster."

Her sister had just come home from a period of incarceration.

Making that card for her sister was probably the most important activity for her that morning.

After Randa checked through her schoolwork, she pointed her in the direction of paper options, and went to grab the markers. Quietly, the girl grabbed a pencil, let out a deep breath and started sketching onto the page. I watched her eyes scan the page, carefully considering where she would write Happy Birthday, and I realized this was more than a break or extracurricular activity. She was still learning.

There are multiple ways of knowing, and of learning how we know what we know.

We know through experiences, images, stories, numbers and statistics, applications, intuition, and a host of other ways. Women have known this for generations—it's the same energy that led our grandmothers to trust the "eyes in the back of their heads" or to suggest that you might "live a long time" if you call someone after they've uttered your name. The energy we produce is powerful, whether we recognize it or not. It is at once delicate and durable, part of a human connection that we sometimes forget to nurture.

Girls on the margins witness and practice, through the blues, various forms of self-preservation and ways of knowing. Coping strategies, especially ones that are dangerous, like self-harming, are perceived by schools, parents, and concerned community members as vices, and they can certainly interrupt school and disrupt a girl's healing process. However, using art as a way to address pain can lead girls through grief, loss, and trauma in ways that can facilitate healing.

When language doesn't quite reach the destination sought by survivors, art therapy can allow one's deepest understandings, fears, joys, and opportunities to be revealed. Music therapy, the most researched medium of the healing arts, has been shown to soothe stress, decrease anxiety, restore emotional balance, and effectively stimulate auditory function to abolish or control pain.[27] Visual arts have been associated with providing refuge from "intense emotions associated with illness."[28] Researcher Nia Nunn suggested that models to uplift strength and sadness in Black girlhood (such as art) can become an important intervention, stating, "The concept of Super-Girl provides a metaphor that illustrates the balance and imbalance of multiple social constructs."[29] Teaching practices that integrate these strategies into the activities of the classroom may also pull girls from the margins into an intentionally liberative learning space.

⌒

"Draw a picture of an apple," Dawn, a therapist and art instructor said to a group of girls. "I don't want it to be recognizable. Make the picture *really* bad."

In a meeting convened by National Crittenton,* girls from seven states—Washington, California, Kansas, Colorado, New York, Mississippi, and Oregon—convened in Portland to discuss ACEs early one summer morning. In the meeting, Dawn led the group through an exercise that began to uplift processes that

---

* National Crittenton (www.nationalcrittenton.org) is a 135-year-old national organization with a mission to "catalyze social systems change for girls and young women impacted by chronic adversity, violence, and injustice."

could be engaged in classrooms to encourage the type of connections that facilitate self-love. The girls had already completed an exercise where they were to write in pencil or marker the things that other people say about them. Each quickly covered the large sheet of paper in words and phrases that represented the lowest moments in her young life.

Some of the girls wrote words and phrases like "sinner," "too young to be a mom," and "They say I'm fat." Others wrote, "They say I'm a victim" or "I'm a fighter" and "I have a bad attitude."

"Now, take some paint," Dawn said, once the girls were done, "and cover those words with what you *want* people to say about you."

The girls grabbed the paintbrushes and began to cover the page with new, redemptive language that they felt better reflected who they actually were. Some girls wrote, "Great" or Strong"; others, "Life Changer," "Thick," or "Brave."

I recognized that the girls were open to the exercise, and now even open to a deeper level of conversation about what it meant to live with trauma and how it might impede their development as persons and young scholars. Their faces relaxed as they wrote the new words; some even joked with their neighbors or moved over to sit next to me and other adults.

"Okay, now, on these sheets, I want you to draw happiness," Dawn said, slowly walking around the table of young women and girls, who began to draw images onto blank white sheets of paper. After a few moments passed, she said, "Now draw anger—whatever that looks like for you."

Every head was down, while pens and markers went to work on the paper. Dawn went on to request a few more artistic renditions of feelings before she clarified that no art was "bad" and that honest communication was the only requirement for participating.

"As long as it's honest, it's perfect," she reminded the girls.

Once she had reached an agreement with them about how to evaluate the quality of their work, she led them through an exercise of creating mandalas* and asked each of the girls to draw what "love" looked like to her. Once each girl had finished her own picture, she was to draw the exact same image on the other girls' mandalas, until they became a visual representation of the love that was in that room and in that conversation.

When the girls finished, Dawn asked them what they noticed about the collection of images before them, calling attention to the new images that now adorned their original drawings. "What did you learn from this exercise?" Dawn finally asked after leading a debrief with the girls. "What do you want to say to your younger self?"

These were girls with ACEs scores at the highest levels, survivors of systemic and individual oppression, and yet the pedagogical thrust of blues women helped them make themselves available for learning and personal development.

They knew what people called them, but they also knew what they wanted to be. That truth was at the center of their learning that day. Their truth was a power that could manifest according to their rhythm, in their time, in their key. They understood

---

* A mandala is a symbol of the universe, represented as a diagram, a circle in a square geometric pattern. Rooted in Hinduism and Buddhism, the mandala is often used to establish sacred space or launch intentional transitions toward personal growth.

their struggles and sacrifices as part of a greater experience, a unique one. The complexity of their own stories was the foundation for every interaction with their teachers, program leaders, and peers. It was also the foundation for their ability to transcend their pain and repurpose it for their well-being. Hiding it only led to dangerous coping mechanisms. Centering it allowed them to engage in honest exchanges to facilitate healing. From their own words, I created this poem:

Call me . . .
A Leader
Mature
Different
Independent
Headstrong
Overachiever
Smart
Thick
Sophisticated
Wise
name
Beyoncé.[30]

"In order to grow, you have to take care of your roots," one girl said. "Don't hold on to the things that you know weigh you down."

Interlude
"Dance Is My Spirit Language"

Freedom.

That's the word that comes up for me when I think about dance—a space to just let go. This English isn't even our people's soul spirit language. It's a language that was imposed on us, and there are so many ways in which it's so rigid.

Sometimes young people say, "Oh, they *looked* at me funny. I don't like how they *looked* at me."

Sometimes, we pathologize that. Oh, that's trauma, that's hypervigilance, that's post-traumatic slave syndrome or whatever, and maybe some of that's true; I'm not going to take away from any of those theories. Some of that is useful. But I wonder if it is also acknowledging another way of communicating. Sometimes we do communicate in just looks or in a slight tilt of the shoulder, or a head roll, or a look and a look away. There are ways that we communicate just with the body that young people, at least the Black and Brown girls that I work with, are really attuned to. I think there's so much wisdom in it. They know.

Some of that is about survival. Some of it does come from the idea that in order to be safe, I need to be able to read what is happening with people's bodies. And some of it, I just wonder, if it's, like, communicating beyond words and how important that is.

When I was coming up as a kid, my father was incarcerated. It was a big secret. We didn't talk about it. We were all going through it, but it was a secret. We didn't discuss it. My mom was really focused on us achieving academically, you know, giving us all the things she thought we needed as tools for success, and there was no room to have a deep, emotional experience as it related to my father's incarceration. Dance was a gift I came to this earth with that helped me release so much of the pain related to doing time on the outside with my dad. It started when I was two, my mother took me to *Sesame Street*. She said that Big Bird and them were doing their thing, and I just got up, right up to the base of the stage, and just started dancing as a young girl.

I think dance is my spirit language. It's how I communicate that which I've been told is not okay to communicate. So, for me, it's always been a space where I have felt free. Using music with dance, creating dances to songs that inspired me or spoke truth—like, India.Arie was my everything when I was a teenager. All the ways she was speaking about loving yourself, and just the way she spoke—the wisdom—really resonated with me, and I made up so many dances to her music. I think dance is a place of freedom.

Also, a place for sexual freedom. . . . Coming up in a socially conservative Christian household, and also a household of trauma, sex was taboo and also painful to talk about. As I was coming of age in my sexuality, dancehall and hip-hop and whining . . . they were a way of expressing my sexuality, especially as I got older and studied their roots in African dance. Learning about this whole womb part of our bodies, the hips and everything—there's so much power! And creative energy is held there. So *yes!* To being connected to that part of our bodies. *Yes!* To being connected to our sexuality, because there's so much power there. Colonization has divorced us from that part of ourselves and shamed us for being connected to that part of us. That impacts the girls, Black girls who want to express their sexuality but are shamed for it, when really, there's so much power there for them. How do we teach them to be aware of that in a way that honors them and isn't victimizing or full of shame?

We create spaces where people can just be free. One example with the Black Girls Matter work that's happening in Miami—the young people were really clear that yes, they want to organize, and yes, they want to get political wins, yes, they want to change things that are going on with the schools, but they also just want to have fun and be free—and that's also radical and revolutionary for them.

And so we're like, "Yes, that should happen."

Some of the programming that we do includes "kickbacks" and chill sessions. We had a Candy and Consent Valentine's Day party. It was just a party, and there were signs up about consent, and there was an elevator pitch about consent that the young people did from the DJ box, and the DJ made some announcements, but really, it was a party. Just giving them a chance to twerk and be free. Framing it as "Candy and Consent" allowed them the freedom to not have to worry—or at least to know that they could worry less—about being touched inappropriately, and without being body-shamed. They created a container, with the support of adult allies, in which they could be free to dance, and be wild, and get on the floor, and sweat—everything that they wanted. It was a space that doesn't often exist for them.

Tanisha "Wakumi" Douglas
S.O.U.L. Sisters Leadership Collective
Florida/New York

Track 5

Shake Hands with the Devil, Make Him Crawl in the Sand

Exploring Restorative Solutions

I'm gonna do something for you, ain't never been done.
I'm gonna hold back the lightning with the palm of my hand,
Shake hands with the devil, make him crawl in the sand.
I'm a woman, oh yeah!

> —*Ellas McDaniel (Bo Diddley) and Koko Taylor,*
> *"I'm a Woman" (Alligator Records, 1978)*

"**W**ho wrote this book?" I heard a woman's voice ask. It was like thunder—strong and raspy. It didn't take long for me to realize that it belonged to the woman who had waved in my direction from the entrance to the hotel's ballroom.

I was preparing to deliver a keynote address for a restorative justice conference in Rochester, New York, when I glanced across the room and spotted a tall, Afro Latina woman with the complexion of raw honey, surrounded by a small group of teen girls—Black and Latina—who were throwing up their fists in a power salute. I thought she intended it for someone else until I found her approaching me, waving a copy of *Pushout* and demanding to know the author.

"I did," I answered, standing from my seat to meet her.

"I thought so," she paused, took a breath, and said, "I just want to thank you."

Then she flung her arms around my body, embracing me with a tight squeeze. I could feel her anxiety, her gratitude, and her love.

"I came to ask you to sign my book," she said. "And this."

The woman dropped a large manila envelope onto the table. I glanced down at it, but I didn't touch it. Instead, I listened to her as she introduced me to the dark brown girl standing beside her. I quietly admired the girl's large Afro puff.

"That's my niece," she said. "She's on a five-day suspension. Her principal is here."

She rolled her eyes. The irony of our being at a restorative justice conference—an intervention that is supposed to be offered *instead* of a suspension—wasn't lost on any of us.

I looked at her niece, who offered a shy smile.

"That school has no idea what's going on," the woman muttered. "I understand what's going on because that was *me*. They have no idea what we have to go through."

I nodded. While I didn't know her or her niece's personal stories, I knew enough, having heard hundreds of pushout stories, to know that the woman and the girl who stood before me had experiences that would likely produce a set of very high ACEs scores.

"Open it," the woman demanded.

Confused, I looked back at her.

"The envelope," she said. "Open it."

Inside the envelope was a twenty-five-page criminal conviction record. I thumbed through it and saw enough to know that
the woman in front of me had received—and initiated—a great
deal of harm.

"Your book," she said. "This was the first book I read where I
could see myself. I want you to sign it."

I was accustomed to being asked to sign, but this was the first
time anyone had asked me to sign a copy of her criminal record,
and honestly, I didn't want to do it. That record was a symbol of
all the things that had gone wrong—all the ways in which her
trauma had triggered responses that were violations of law, violations of trust, and violations of the sacred human condition.
Looking back at the woman in front of me, it was clear that all
of these things were part of a distant—yet nagging—past. But I
understood why she wanted me to sign it. A criminal conviction
history is often the result of school pushout—and in her case,
it was. It was a path that she did not want her niece to repeat.
That's why she dragged her niece out on a Saturday morning
to join five hundred other people, mostly deeply committed
educators, at a daylong restorative justice conference. She was
seeking an alternative for her niece and for her past self. Asking
me to sign her conviction history had to be her way of making
sense of a criminalization that followed her unresolved trauma
and conflict—the outcome of relationships stunted by neglect
and abuse.

I looked at the paper for a while and then decided to write

"You are so much more than this" before signing my name. She read it, smiled, and we hugged again.

That criminal record was a reflection of where this woman had been, not who she was when I met her or who she will be in the future. Later that morning, I learned that this woman was receiving an award for her community organizing and leadership. Rochester's restorative justice leadership saw the same thing in her that I did. When called to the stage, she grabbed her niece's hand and they marched up together. Just past the stairs, the two of them stopped and thrust their fists in the air.

There was that power salute again.

"Stop the pushout!" she yelled and continued across the stage with her niece.

She is restorative justice, I thought. *This is the work.*

⌒

Restorative justice is an alternative paradigm designed to repair harm between and among people, and between people and institutions. Instead of a focus on punishing someone for a harmful act or letting that act be used by authorities to further isolate her, "restorative" (or "transformative") approaches seek to identify the harm, determine what needs to be done to repair it, and agree on whose obligation it is to do it. In *Pushout*, I explored the idea that restorative approaches might work on not just interpersonal connections, but also relationships between individuals and institutions. This is particularly important to Black and Brown girls, for whom educational institutions might have been part of the tapestry of harm.

One issue with restorative approaches is that schools interpret them with a wide range of variability. One school might consider in-school suspension and community-service clean-up restorative. Another might consider its peer court, however punitive the outcomes, restorative. Yet another might run circles—wherein those involved in conflict sit together in guided conversation about the harm and how best to respond to it—as its primary restorative practice. Program fidelity and uniformity is often a challenge, though there are resources to support it.[1]

Baltimore Public Schools, a district where the majority of the female student population is African American—began its first restorative conferences in schools in 1997. It is one strategy that the school district has implemented to address its history of criminalizing Black youth and other students impacted by violence and victimization. To make steady moves toward becoming a "restorative practices district," which normalizes the use of restorative circles as a primary response to student conflict, is a promising approach. The excitement around this effort, however difficult in the competing climate of increased police presence in schools nationwide, is palpable. One of the first studies I participated in, which focused on the conditions of Black girls, took place in Baltimore. At that time, officers in schools were concerned about girls' expressions of sexuality and the fights that seemed to emerge from having to mask their identities.

"The girls are fighting over other *girls*," one officer whispered to me.

I frowned at his homophobia, but focused my attention on the truth from the girls. Little had been done at that time to make girls feel safe to be themselves, which—by the girls' own admission—led to other conflicts. Cultures of violence normalize fighting as a valid response to harm. Responding to student conflict through restorative approaches felt like a great solution then, and as it spreads through the district, it remains exciting.

The district engages proactive circles to improve the school climate, reactive circles to resolve conflict, and informal restorative practices and affective statements that prioritize informal engagements between educators and students throughout the school year. Research on the effort as it is developing show preliminary outcomes that are promising, not only in terms of reducing suspensions, but also in terms of facilitating mental health for its student participants. In response to a survey study led by the Open Society Institute in Baltimore, one respondent said, "Restorative practices as a conflict resolution technique would allow students to be more aware of their behaviors and the impacts, on others and themselves," describing this effect as "empathy restoration" in schools.[2]

Although there are many ways to repair harm and build relationships, many restorative approaches have been reduced to a single modality—the circle—or to a peer "conferencing" option that has led to a limited lens through which to address the harm or pain at the root of the conflict. But this is a *challenge*—not a deal breaker. Words can express a lot, and when they are used with greatest impact, they can transform an individual's perception of herself and others who share space in the world around her. The trick is creating the premium conditions for this transformation to occur—opening up the conditions for restorative spaces in education and justice systems, rather than condensing them.

community service hours, and treatment with community resources if necessary.

I had an opportunity to observe a case involving a twenty-four-year-old migrant woman from Guatemala, who had been driving under the influence. She entered the conference room where everyone was assembled dressed in a printed sheath dress and pumps. Her long black hair swayed against her back as she walked in, greeted everyone, and promptly took a seat. She sat upright in the seat, tucked her legs under the chair, and placed her hands squarely on her lap. A graduate student who lived with her thirty-eight-year-old mother and forty-six-year-old father, this was her first offense.

"We're not here to judge or scold. We leave that for the ordinary courts," the judge said to open her circle. "This program is to establish what was the harm and how we will repair it."

The group included the judge, the young woman, two public defenders, a psychologist, and a police officer, who represented the "community" affected by the incident. They began by sharing introductions, establishing the rules and guidelines for the circle, explaining use of the talking piece, a small ornament held by the person whose turn it is to speak. They agreed to engage in active listening throughout the process.

Then the psychologist asked, "Can you tell us what happened?" She handed the talking piece to the young woman.

The young woman proceeded to describe what happened—that she normally does not drink, that she'd had too much to drink at a friend's house and then tried to drive home. She crashed into a parked car and became terrified as witnesses of the incident, and the car's owner, emerged to berate her. No

⌢

In 2018, Costa Rica joined a growing number of countries w.
a national law implementing restorative justice (conferencin,
restitution, and community service) as the primary approacl
to first-time, low-level violations. Restorative conferencing and
healing circles had been used in classrooms for decades. In some
countries, like New Zealand and Canada, it has been in place
long enough to produce global evidence of its effectiveness,[3] but
its formal inclusion in the judicial process is still relatively new
globally. Restorative practices are a paradigm shift in the global
concept of justice and are being applied in South Africa, Nigeria,
Ghana, Mexico, El Salvador, Guatemala, Colombia, Italy, and
Spain, as well as the United States. Restorative justice in schools,
commonly cited as having early roots in Australia, has produced
similarly positive effects in reducing criminalization and cycles
of harm,[4] and the application of these practices in the legal system is instructive for learning spaces that now seek to transition
from punishment to restoration.

In Costa Rica's legal system, there are a series of public fil-
ters to determine the viability of a case, which is used to assess
the potential for a person who has caused harm to enter the
process. Admission of legal responsibility, cognitive ability to
make sound decisions, and the ability to negotiate and reach an
agreement are all prerequisites. Once an agreement is reached,
it goes before judicial review, and the person who has caused
harm participates in a "high-control–high-support" process in
which they are called upon to follow through with their agreement. Typically, the resolution involves restitution payments,

one was physically harmed, but the owner of the car demanded payment. It was more than she could afford. When she did not immediately consent to pay the car owner's demand, someone called the police and she was arrested.

"What happened after the incident?" the psychologist asked.

"Then, they put me in a dungeon for eight hours," she said.

When asked to describe what the harms were in this scenario, the young woman said, "Someone's car was hit, . . . and I was taken to a dungeon. My freedoms were dependent on someone else."

Her admission was followed by comments from the police officer, who described the dangers of driving drunk and the potential harm to the community.

The session included the opportunity for everyone to address the potential impact of the young woman's actions, how she felt, and her interests in community-service work. In the end, it was agreed that she would spend 120 hours over two years volunteering in a home for the elderly, and that she would pay $450 in restitution. She was advised that if she did not comply with the terms of the agreement, the privilege of the restorative approach would be revoked and she would then have to participate in the traditional legal process.

The young woman understood the terms and concluded by saying, "I am very sorry. . . . I am doing this because of a mistake I made."

Following the meeting, I watched as the legal team sat with the young woman to finalize the paperwork. They all seemed very pleased with the proceedings. The judge, now sitting behind a desk with a computer, plugged their agreements into a long legal document that would bind her to the verbal agreements she made during the circle. The incident, upon completion, would be sealed and would not negatively affect her prospects of completing her education or finding employment and housing. As the judge and legal team continued their work to wrap up the meeting, the young woman stared blankly out of the open door. Deep in thought, her wide eyes glazed over, cementing a solemn expression made only graver by the sound of rain tapping against the windows. She sat silently and waited for everyone to complete the paperwork. Once the sheets were printed, she carefully looked them over and, with pursed lips, picked up a pen to sign her name in agreement.

"This is twenty-first-century justice," the judge later said to me and the group that I was with. "I know it is thousands of years old, but here in Costa Rica, this is twenty-first-century justice."

Indeed, there was a lot right with this approach. The victim—the car owner, in this case—chose to be represented by the community police officer, who faced the young woman and participated in a conversation about ways to reconcile the wrong and repair the harm. In this case, as in 96 percent of the cases that were processed by the Restorative Justice office in this country, the victim was happy with the agreement. Instead of forcing the person who caused harm to spend time in jail or default on fees and payments she couldn't afford, it focused on her strengths and provided an opportunity for those strengths to be used in service to the community she harmed. Also, instead of the resolution process taking a year, which can happen if the situation moves through the traditional legal process, it took about a month.

In a meeting with one of the psychologists, I mentioned that possibly outside of the scope of expertise for the legal team was the reality that this young woman had *also* faced a harm from being incarcerated for eight hours in a dungeon. Presented as a consequence rather than a harm, her incarceration was treated as a deterrent from ever driving under the influence again. And maybe it will be just that—but unresolved trauma of any kind, especially in association with another act of harm, still has consequences that require our attention. She closed her eyes and nodded, acknowledging that at times our best efforts to resolve harm using restorative practices are still located adjacent to— and sometimes within—systems that produce harm, consciously and unconsciously.

When the practice of restoring relationships fails to acknowledge its proximity to institutions that facilitate harm, we fail to acknowledge the ways in which the process itself benefits, or is tainted by, the privilege of coercion. This is the square inside of the circle. If the policy is to use restorative approaches as an alternative to punitive discipline—in any context—then we must, as a global community, consider ways to excise violence from the *process* of making one eligible for participation in these programs and strategies.

Elsewhere in Costa Rica, this was a work in progress.

In schools, restoring relationships with other people or institutions requires that girls be willing to repair the most important relationship of all—the one with themselves. Educators' ability to create conditions of safety requires an understanding of the many ways to "restore" or "repair," while remembering that fostering love for girls is how we lay the groundwork for transformation.

All over the globe, elevating the visibility of girls and young women in conversations about educational equity is a struggle. In Nigeria, advocates shared the pain of knowing that hundreds of girls have been kidnapped from school and forced into nonconsensual marriage. In India, I was told by an academic that school pushout was familiar to girls in his community. In England, a journalist shared with me that Black girls were often experiencing barriers to their full inclusion in rigorous educational programs. In Australia, a teacher shared with me that she was mapping emergent trends regarding the Black and Latinx girls in her school for incarcerated and systems-involved youth. In Costa Rica, I was told by an educator that "girls are hard to reach." The truth is that race and gender mediates how we see and respond to youth on the margins.

In many societies, though girls may be protected by law from violence, the programming on the ground or in the community has not been created to meet the need. In whispers, people may acknowledge the various ways vulnerable girls are being underserved. Yet because of the visibility of boys—especially in places where the proximal "boy trouble" overshadows that of the girls, the needs of girls may be obscured. For that reason, many of the examples of promising efforts toward restorative approaches have been implemented only with boys and young men—even though many women also have a need for alternative paradigms of accountability to harm. There are, however, promising models with boys in trouble with the law, which may inform the work with their female counterparts.

Surgir means "to emerge" in Spanish, and Organización Surgir is a restorative alternative to incarceration for young men and boys in Costa Rica. Led by educators, social workers, and psychologists who have been trained in strategies to help young people repair relationships and advance in school, the program has developed a restorative educational model. They work to develop an educational plan for young people who have faced extraordinary trauma; the majority of participants are childhood sexual assault survivors or victims (and sometimes perpetrators) of violence. Students meet regularly with counselors and social workers to help them manage their housing and occupational needs, and educators work closely with the public school system to ensure that students can learn better and make up lost credits toward their graduation from high school.

"Everyone cannot be a teacher in this program," Surgir's director said during a meeting with local psychologists and justice system stakeholders. She emphasized that teachers need to be trained in restorative justice and accept the idea that there is resilience in the educational process. This is a fundamental aspect of teaching for liberation—uplifting resilience as an inherent human asset. Engaging strategies to learn, even after a mistake has been made, is how resilience becomes a path to freedom and high performance, rather than a path to hardened emotions. To restore relationships under these circumstances may mean imagining a reality that has never been in place.

The critical part of this model—and the piece that may hold the most promise of transferability to Black and Brown girls—is in the idea of creating an "academic legacy." The program helps its students chart their own truths and progress, allowing them to design how what they learn shapes the way others understand them and their stories for future generations. Recognizing this provides an opportunity for their education to be more than a personal exercise. When education is connected to a broader purpose, it can be nurtured as an act of social justice. This is especially important for Black and Brown girls, who often thrive in a spirit of connectivity and relationships.

Foundations for Transformation

Fear is the enemy of innovation and creativity. Being fearful of a new practice—even if it is actually quite old, tried, and true—can produce systems and practices that exacerbate harm rather than mitigate it. Those who respond to harm by addressing needs must respond to the needs of the person *causing* harm, as well as those of the person harmed and the community. This is a fundamental paradigm shift that can be hard for even the most stalwart progressive to grasp, especially if it requires us to rethink conventional notions of accountability. In the United States, a growing number of schools have adopted restorative approaches to working with students in conflict.[5] Some schools have used restorative approaches to build community *before* there is a conflict. Even though U.S. schools still overwhelmingly use excessive and exclusionary discipline, more holistic responses are gaining popularity, likely because the schools that adopt them experience less conflict and more safety.

In a review of the research literature on restorative justice, conducted by national nonprofit WestEd, the authors point to two specific considerations for educators interested in establishing or developing restorative programs in U.S. schools.[6] These are funding and sustainability. A funded coordinator position helps to grow and maintain the practice. Some districts, such as Detroit Public Schools, leveraged their Title I funding. Other educators have worked with administrators to fundraise through grants or community partnerships, such as Community Works West and Restorative Justice for Oakland Youth, both in Oakland, California. To sustain the project, restorative justice should be integrated into a school and/or district philosophy, both as formal policies and as professional development opportunities.[7]

Schools should also consider implementing an assessment process for recruitment, as well as eligibility criteria for the program. Program criteria that support girls can be developed by asking:

- Are incidents that disproportionately include girls, particularly Black and Brown girls, eligible for participation in the restorative program?
- Are the modalities of the restorative justice program responsive to the needs of girls who have been harmed as well as those doing the harm?
- What considerations are made for survivors of trauma?
- Is there a space for creative expression?
- How can other trusted people "hold space" for them in the process of repairing their relationships with themselves first?
- If girls are resistant to the circle, what preparation can occur to move them toward healing and reconciliation with themselves and others with whom they are in conflict?

Pedagogical practices that acknowledge the harm that has been conducted and then work to repair and/or transform the relationships between learning environments or communities and girls at highest risk of school pushout are those that uplift the most positive aspects of student survival strategies and apply them to student mapping of success. For example, efforts that provide girls with the opportunity to state their own educational goals at the beginning of the year and help them track progress, help to keep youth who would otherwise lose focus be reminded of *why* they pursue scholarship.

Strategies that also offer opportunities for educators to guide students in reflecting on their goals at various stages of the school year help them connect their incremental progress to their greater goals. They can also connect their goals to the goals of their learning "squad," a group of friends and classmates who encourage each other to be accountable to themselves and their learning. It also shifts the question from "How am I doing in school?" as measured by grades toward, "What will be my educational story? How am I doing relative to how I came in and where I'd like to be at the end of the year?" These reflective questions might typically be discussed at home or during parent-teacher conferences, but they are not necessarily part of the discussions that educators have with students who are struggling to build or rebuild their relationship with school and peers. Girls who have been historically marginalized or disconnected from school need constant support, like academic coaching, but also support for learning how schools have caused harm in their lives and communities, and how these institutions will atone. Repairing the relationship between institutions and individuals differs from repairing harm between individuals.

I have asked many judges, lawyers, and educators throughout the United States and in other countries what they believe to be the worldview necessary to build restorative approaches in schools and other institutions of learning. Judges have confirmed that they feel more confident in processes that require youth to engage in activities, and in agreements that develop character better than punishment. Judges I have spoken and worked with have acknowledged that repression is limited in its capacity to respond to harm and that punishment, a form of repression, does little to remedy the root causes of conflict. In order to change, young people need to feel fulfilled by the agreements on how to repair harm.

School leaders who engage in restorative approaches agree: the opportunity to build a strong community can happen only if people who are involved in harm can be part of developing a solution to that harm. What is restored is the *love*. The approach that helps schools become locations for healing also helps them uplift the source of human connectedness. That is the "restorative impulse" that prioritizes a connectedness that we can feel in our movements, our energy, our bones.[8]

The competencies of Black and Brown girls are diverse, and include strategies discussed earlier (intuition and faith-based influences), as well as other cultural traditions that support their healing through discussion ("talking it out"), sports, and art.[9] For educators interested in repairing the relationship between girls of color and institutions, it's time to turn again to the wise words of blues women. When Koko Taylor reimagined Muddy Waters's "Mannish Boy" to write "I'm a Woman," she sang that she could "shake hands with the devil, make him crawl in the sand." Growth sometimes requires coming to terms with the "trickster" aspect of our own identities in order to reconcile and disarm forces that could otherwise be disruptive in our lives. Taking control of one's healing process—or helping someone else with hers—so as to discover one's own force and begin using it for good can forge a pathway toward personal redemption as well as collective promise. From this place can emerge a young woman or girl who can become a leader of self, household, community, industry, and nation.

For educators working with marginalized girls of color in the restorative processes, engaging this paradigm of justice means preparing (and reestablishing after conflict or harm) a climate for optimal human connection and intellectual exchange. Students need the chance to articulate what harm has been committed, its consequences, who is responsible for it, the needs of those involved, and whose obligation it is to respond to these needs. Often the pain that leads to conflict in the first place with girls of color is rooted in other forms of oppression that they have internalized and then outwardly expressed. This is not information that should be used to *excuse* negative behaviors without accountability, but it is an *opportunity* for girls who are fighters or otherwise disruptive to confront themselves, understand their traumas, and overcome the fears at the root of their misbehavior. This elevated level of accountability allows reconciliation without derailing young women and girls from their promise. It redirects their negative energy to positive outcomes without exclusionary discipline and criminalization.

The Mentoring Center, based in Oakland, California, the home of EMERGE, uses what it calls the transformative mentoring model to help girls of color to resolve *internal* conflict before being asked to resolve its harmful external manifestation. Transformative mentoring is "an intensive and long-term, curriculum-based approach that utilizes a specific set of best practices for cognitive restructuring to address issues of positive self-identity, positive youth development, healing and individual and collective transformation."[10] It supports the healthy development of youth who have experienced great harm, helping them be their best selves. According to Celsa Snead, executive director of the Mentoring Center, transformative mentoring is an opportunity to consider not just that there is a whole child at the center of this work, but that the experiences and conditions that make that child who she is should be used to remind her of her greatest potential—to set new standards.

"Transformative mentoring requires us to *know* our children," Celsa said. "And, when we know them and believe in their promise, our approach is grounded in healing. *We* are not transforming the lives of young women. Rather, we know that young women are responsible for transforming their own lives and we support them, in part, by helping them recognize their own sense of agency. We support them in creating their own process, and we are aware of and responsive to each student's individual needs, challenges, talents, skills, strengths, and circumstances."

In *Are Prisons Obsolete?* an exploration of the utility and function of punishment and incarceration, Angela Y. Davis wrote:

> Transforming schools into locations for decarceration such that they "become places that encourage the joy of learning" for Black and Brown requires for us

to transform how schools have been fundamentally approaching students with complex, compounded histories of trauma and victimization.[11]

Making schools "places that encourage the joy of learning" for Black and Brown girls requires us to work together to change how schools approach them as scholars and as people. If we prepare schools to be restorative for the most vulnerable among us, all students—even the least vulnerable—will be well served.

Interlude
"Listen to Them"

They don't want to be told what to do. They want us to listen to them and guide them to follow through with the vision of life they have for themselves. They want to finish school and be supported in that process, so I just show up for them every day and show that I care.

They want us to listen to them, not tell them the things that we want them to do. That's what I wanted in my own life, and that's what I try to do with girls who are now where I was.

The young women tell me, "Miss Randa, even when you're mad at us, you still call us."

That consistency is important. I'm always there.

I show that I care.

That's what is most important.

Randa Powell
The Mentoring Center
EMERGE Educational Reentry Program
California

Track 6

"Today I'm with You . . . Ain't That Some Love"

Building Community Through Volunteerism

I go crazy when you love me.
Got me acting a mess,
Even got the nerve to say I'm better than my mama's
Collards and cornbread, yeah.

> *Nickolas Ashford, Warren Felder, Tiwa Savage,*
> *Valerie Simpson, and Andrew Wansel, "Collard*
> *Greens & Cornbread" as sung by Fantasia*
> *(Fantasia Barrino-Taylor),* Back to Me
> *(J Records, 2010)*

In the mid-1990s, every Friday, I volunteered in a San Francisco public elementary school to teach West African dance

to a group of fifth-grade girls. I still remember how the faces of
the girls would light up when I walked in. Admittedly, I was in a
favored position, a "reward" for girls who completed all of their
work. When I entered the class, they'd immediately start putting
away their books, because "Miss Monique" had arrived to dance
with them. I'd just come from being a competitive performer
with my sorority's step team in New York City, and I cherished
the time to feel my body move in dance.

I began every class by stretching and asking the girls how
their week went. Typically, they would offer versions of "fine"
before pressing me to move on with the choreography. We were
developing a dance to Mamadou Ly's "Fere," a Senegalese drum
beat that begins with a syncopated tune that eventually builds
into a high-energy Mandinka rhythm. We danced—but more
important, we were developing relationships with each other
and having conversations through our bodies that restored our
collective faith in school as a place where such joy was possible.
There the girls could connect to themselves and their roots in a
way that could uplift and reaffirm knowledge of their ancestry
and lineage.

What can a weekly dance class do?

The time we spent together was a participation in the process
of bridging their histories with their present, an opportunity to
raise questions that are critical to a liberative pedagogy. Because
I was not being paid to be there, the girls believed that I *wanted*
to be there. Just knowing that I would give my time to be there
with them spoke volumes about their longing to be received
by their school as worthy of investment. It was a time for them
to freely express their needs by using their bodies rather than

words. But because they felt free in their bodies, they also felt free in their spirits to verbalize the conditions that they felt were causing or contributing to their harm.

One day during the time that we were together, I noticed that the girls were low on energy. When I asked what they'd had for lunch, they shared information about the food at the school. This conversation confirmed that poor nutrition had reduced their intellectual and physical performance. It also informed a meaningful conversation that I was able to have with the primary teacher, who developed strategies to supplement, where she could, her students' nutrition. At the time, I hardly felt empowered to approach the school or the district to address the nutritional needs of its students, but I now recognize that poor nutrition can fuel the increasing involvement of girls in the juvenile court system. I don't know how many of those girls went on to experience suspension, chronic absenteeism, or criminalization, but I do know that their diets were making them more prone to all three.

Healthy food provides the vitamins and other nutrients that the young body needs to grow and thrive. Food has restorative value—some foods have been associated with the release of pheromones that can bring pleasure, but many foods also contain healing properties. And better nutrition can be a decarceration strategy. Overall, violent behavior—whether or not associated with food neglect—is more prevalent among boys than girls,[1] but for girls, being hungry can trigger actions of poor impulse control and violence. Research on the biology of antisocial behaviors (which are typically associated with incarceration) show that girls who are experiencing hunger are more inclined to respond to their conditions of poverty with participation in the underground economies—particularly stealing, survival sex, and sometimes sexual exploitation.[2] They are also more likely to experience discipline in schools if their thinking is impaired by food insecurity. A food-insecure household is one without enough food for an active and healthy life for all its members. For women, food insecurity is associated with obesity, anxiety, depression, risky sex, poor coping strategies, and negative pregnancy outcomes.[3] These are all conditions that degrade academic performance as well as the ability to make healthy economic and life choices.

And food is love. Good love, when it's tasty.

Black and Brown girls disproportionately experience persistent food insecurity in the United States,[4] but schools are already emergent as healing spaces in this regard. Thanks in part to robust advocacy to improve the quality of food in public schools, many young people now eat well-balanced meals there. Even as recent public policy has sought to dismantle school nutrition programs, many schools are working with their communities to fill in the gaps. Blessings in a Backpack[5] and the Feeding America BackPack[6] Program are two examples of national anti-hunger initiatives that rely on volunteers to help schools remain food resources for children during the academic calendar, over weekends, and even in the summer months. These are important strategies for all children in need, but because of the disproportionate degree to which girls of color experience food insecurity, it has a particular impact on them.

Schools with the resources have started their own gardens or participated in the cultivation of community gardens that teach youth to grow their own organic vegetables. Tens of thousands of schools operate a learning garden, connecting this work with science and arts curricula and, in some cases, using work in the community garden as give-back opportunities for restorative justice. Since 1982, KidsGardening—the leading nonprofit agency working to bring gardening to schools—has reached more than ninety thousand school garden educators each month, supporting their volunteer recruitment, training, and retention efforts through webinars, printed pamphlets, and digital resources.[7] Of course, volunteerism can include more than getting your hands dirty in a garden or leading a dance class in an elementary school. It's more than bake sales and tutoring services.

Black and Brown parents and community members give in many ways that support the culture of a school for their girls. They feed girls, give them rides, provide counsel in moments of crisis, mentor, give hugs, allow girls to "crash" on their couches, and routinely include them among the community of "babies" for which they advocate. These activities are typically undervalued and unreported in the traditional ways of tracking involvement in schools, because they are not called "volunteering" or "service-learning" as much as they are treated simply as "being there" for young people. Whether they personally know these girls or not, the love is real. These are values that have long been associated with the social movements for justice in this country—the overwhelming majority of civil rights organizational membership is volunteer.

The NAACP, the nation's oldest and largest civil rights organization, has more than five hundred thousand volunteer members,[8] and UnidosUS (formerly the National Council of La Raza) boasts a constituency of about three hundred affiliate community organizations.[9] Other groups, such as the National Urban League, the Mexican American Legal Defense and Educational Fund, Black Lives Matter, and the Black Youth Project 100, bring volunteer membership for Black and Brown well-being to millions of people, who could become effective conduits for educational justice that intentionally benefits Black and Brown girls. Members of these groups are all individuals who are concerned about their communities, and many of these organizations have developed robust educational-justice agendas, which include a call for volunteerism and connection with schools. Working with these organizations to align interest may lead to sustainable partnerships that increase resources for a school or learning community. Likewise, Black, Latinx, and Indigenous professional, civic, cultural, and fraternal organizations are filled with volunteers who value education and who are often in key positions to negotiate partnerships that could have a positive impact on Black and Brown girls. These resources for schools are often untapped.

Like teaching and learning, volunteerism is a partnership—an agreement premised on trust. Teachers must trust that the volunteers are able to support their instruction with students; volunteers must trust the teachers and students to guide their activities toward the best outcomes for the culture of the classroom, and the students must entrust their learning to the teachers and volunteers. Weaknesses in these relationships are easily revealed and result in poor performance outcomes for the girls.

In my interactions with school leaders and educators throughout the country, I have asked how volunteers could best be used. The overwhelming majority of those I've spoken with expressed some desire for help in maintaining a culture of learning and development in the classroom. This might include mentorship and tutoring, but some educators need specialists to help young women form healthy relationships. According to an elementary school teacher in New York City, very young girls often exhibit "mean girl" behaviors early, because they are being socialized in part by reality TV. Volunteers could "help model language and behavior where words are thoughtful," especially during times of conflict. For this teacher, it would be helpful to have volunteers "model behavior that encourages an appreciation for learning and a growth mind-set."

The African proverb "Sticks in a bundle are unbreakable" suggests that a community effort has more impact than an individual one. The sticks are not as strong individually as when they come together. Rather than interpreting the work of education as a matter of the individual, it's important to involve the extended community. When education is a collective experience, the sticks are unbreakable. Expanding the number of people who show up for our girls builds a community that can stand with them in their most vulnerable moments—and stand with teachers struggling to develop transformative relationships with them.

Sometimes the partnerships emerge from unlikely places. For example, the National Black Women's Justice Institute partnered with then Boston city councilor Ayanna Pressley to develop a project that centers girls of color from Roxbury in discussions about access to equitable education. Each year, Councilor Pressley has sponsored a Jump into Peace event, which provided her with an opportunity to host a Double Dutch jump-rope exhibition as an occasion for the community to gather and heal from gender-based violence.

"I started this event because I remember jumping rope as one of the only times during my childhood when I truly felt free," she announced to the crowd that had assembled in Malcolm X Park in Roxbury for the 2017 event.

I knew what she meant. Instantly, I was taken back to my Double Dutch days—jumping on sidewalks and in schoolyards to the chants of, "One up! Two, three, four, five, six, seven, eight, nine. Two up!" For me, too, it was one of the few times in my youth that I felt truly free.

Along the perimeter of the open, outdoor basketball court were a series of organizations, including community-based healing organizations, such as the Louis D. Brown Peace Institute, and public agencies, such as the Boston Medical Center. And, of course, there were the jumpers, the Rope Burners Double Dutch team. Organizations passed out pamphlets and engaged in conversations with community members to share information about domestic and sexual violence. People led healing activities or sat on benches or the basketball court and ate.

To the beat of "Double Dutch Bus," a 1981 funk hit by Frankie Smith, girls began to jump through the ropes, alternating between simple and more complicated tricks that showcased their agility, focus, and connectedness.

Double Dutch bus coming down the street,
Moving pretty fast, so kinda shuffle your feet.

Girls jump-stepped through the two ropes as the turners kept rhythm. Some of the younger ones jumped once with both feet, then kicked one leg out.

"Yeah!" "Hey!" The crowd punctuated each move with affirmations of their greatness.

The smaller girls were followed by the teen girls, who entered to "Poison," an R&B/Hip Hop song by Roxbury's own Bell Biv DeVoe.

Situation is serious.

The girls danced a choreographed piece and then went into a Double Dutch routine that included handstands, splits, and kicks.

"All right now!" "Wooo!" The crowd was right there with them.

At that moment, I realized that this city council member had sponsored one of the most culturally competent and gender-responsive community events I had ever attended—in the name of healing and educational equity for girls. In community with nonprofit organizations, private corporations, city government, and public agencies, people had come together to promote educational justice and an end to gender-based violence, using Double Dutch as its anchor. In this space, we announced the participatory, youth-centered research partnership that would ultimately produce recommendations for Boston-area schools to better respond to the needs of Black and Brown girls.[10]

In 2019, City Councilor Pressley became *Congresswoman* Pressley.

The community got it.

Foundations for Transformation

Volunteerism is about making schools—and the learning and healing that take place there—part of the community, and vice versa. Every school—whether public, private, charter, parochial, or independent—can form community partnerships for engagements responsive to Black and Brown girls.

Paulo Freire said, "The more educators and the people inves-tigate the people's thinking, and are thus jointly educated, the more they continue to investigate. Education and thematic investigation, in the problem-posing concept of education, are simply different moments of the same process."[11]

The question is not so much whether volunteering is appropri-ate and useful. It's how to ensure that the volunteer efforts in a school actually work to support healing and learning for girls of color. Working with organized volunteers to support Black and Brown girls requires the development of activities in partner-ship with the girls. Many times, organized volunteers have their own agenda, which may or may not be appealing to girls who are teetering between inclusion and disengagement in the school. It is important to include specific conversations with leaders of school communities and classrooms to ensure that there is an alignment of goals, objectives, and activities that can support positive academic and social emotional outcomes.

The volunteer program goals, objectives, and activities must be transferrable while maintaining their individual focus. The work to build a sustainable space in each of these categories is ultimately about increasing the capacity for this cross-cultural and cross-agency alignment. Having conversations about the cultural competency *and* gender-responsiveness of a volunteer program's approach are important first steps to establishing whether the program will have its intended impact with Black and Brown girls. Have a good look at the program's printed and digital materials to determine whether there is an intentional, demonstrated commitment to girls of color. Once this program-matic focus is established, there are several important considerations, according to whether these are public school volunteer programs or individually coordinated efforts by parents and community partners.

Public School Volunteer Programs

There are thousands of school volunteer programs active in U.S. public and private schools. They are designed to foster community involvement and support for the schools. Typically, these programs include outreach and coordination of volunteers through private, public, and nonprofit entities. The problem is that many of these programs become more of a numbers game measured by how many volunteers were placed in the classroom to do various tasks rather than by actual effectiveness in improving outcomes among marginalized girls.

Genuine partnerships with private-sector companies toward the positive educational performance of girls of color requires that these companies be "good neighbors" in the sense that they do not cause harm in other facets of these girls' lives. Companies that routinely participate in discriminatory practices or facilitate economic exploitation of communities of color while attempting to partner with schools are engaging in deception and hypocrisy that is transparent to girls who live on the margins or in poverty-stricken families. They may initially welcome the participation of individuals from these companies in the classroom, but they will ultimately use this company's overarching practices as a litmus test for whether their investment in Black and Brown girls is real.

In the development of practices to facilitate freedom for girls of color, the validity of the investment will ultimately be determined by whether it is lasting, sustainable, and extendable. This means that a public school–private sector partnership is not just about how much money a school receives from a given company, but the extent to which the investment reflects broader practices that benefit the communities these girls are growing up in and may lead someday. If these companies have caused harm in the past, has there been a transparent process for reconciliation and remedy? Do these companies include women of color in leadership positions? Do they provide second-chance employment opportunities, hiring qualified people despite a criminal record? Do they practice pay equity? Do they provide childcare or support flexible work schedules responsive to the needs of working mothers?

Partnerships with nonprofit, civic, and faith organizations that specialize in gender-responsive programming must be evaluated by the same criteria as a private-sector investment. An additional consideration for nonprofit agencies is that of the organization's mission. Nonprofits that allow their employees to volunteer in schools or establish partnerships with schools should consider their unique position in serving the public interest. If the nonprofit's mission is to engage in charitable acts, how does it ensure that its employees are volunteering to help increase capacity among the girls to be leaders, and not operating to "save" them? Training matters, as does the structure of the volunteer program.

⌒

Community leaders who facilitate meetings, conferences, and other gatherings often close with a "circle of hope." This exercise requires that individuals form a circle by standing together. Shoulders touching, people face each other across the circle. While it can be uncomfortable in our modern society to be this close, the intention is to work through this challenge and learn to be in community. Circle participants are then asked to turn in the same direction so that they are staring into the back of the head of the person in front of them. They then reach an arm out into the center of the circle and form a fist with the thumb sticking out. Each person grabs the thumb of the person next to her until there is an unbroken circle. Participants are then asked to reflect upon the symbolism of this circle. Often, people approach the formation of the circle with fear of closeness, of vulnerability. But it's the commitment to work through these issues that gives the circle its *hope*.

Volunteer communities are circles of hope as praxis. Schools with a robust volunteer community are a resource for personal and community development. If the circle of hope depends on the commitment to release one's insecurities in order to believe in the power of collective responsibility, then it must also entrust the realization of that belief to all who are affected by the process. Understanding that a pedagogy for the freedom of Black and Brown girls includes more than teachers is foundational. The song we sing is intended for harmonization, and the dance a collaboration.

Blues women couldn't wait, and neither can we. The issues facing our vulnerable girls are urgent. Instead of shying away from their challenges, engage them. Seek to understand who they are and to envision whom they can become. The tempo of this pedagogy is liberation, and its groove is love. Let it light the path to learning for all of us.

Coda

Bomba!

I had an opportunity to visit the Taller Tambuyé dance and drum studio in Old San Juan, Puerto Rico, during a conference on educational justice in 2018. I was there with a group of about twenty other scholars, organizers, and advocates, convened by a funding partner to improve strategies and practices for educational justice. The workshop was intended to give us information about the history of *bomba*, a Puerto Rican style of communal music and dance based on use of the barrel drum. We learned why the drums are built from rum barrels (honoring the roots of the music as developed by Africans on sugar plantations) and how the art is preserved in modern-day Puerto Rico. The dancers begin by performing one at a time, and we learned about the relationship between the dancer—typically a woman—and the drummers, usually men. However, the Tambuyé troupe features female drummers and male dancers, so as to resist notions of power historically left unchallenged in the art form. It was all intellectually stimulating—and then we danced.

I was dancing beside my daughter. Others had brought their children and siblings with them as well. We moved closer together, then farther apart, working in and around each other's space in laughter and syncopation. The

African-inspired movement quickly connected us in waves
that amplified for me the words of Nikki Giovanni in her
poem "Revolutionary Dreams" when she wrote that if she
did what she does "when she's natural," she'd "have a revo-
lution."[1] Sweat beading our foreheads and feet becoming
sore, we all participated in the labor of knowing the history
of Puerto Rico, in the movement to retain one's self in the
context of oppression.

Then the magic happened.

Dancing with us had been two-year-old Aquilah, her
angelic little body weaving between the adult bodies
around her to make her presence known. She was wearing
a pink dress, with a matching bow peeking out from her
tiny, tightly coiled Afro. She was the only dancer under five
years old until Luna, the daughter of the primo drummer
and lead dancer, arrived with her own contributions. She
walked in with bright brown eyes, her loose curls formed
into an Afro. When they found each other, Aquilah and
Luna instantly decided to be friends. One spoke English,
the other Spanish, but they understood their common language and used it to bond in an ancestral legacy of dance.

They hugged each other, laughed, and then hit the dance
floor. Aquilah's pink dress was now covered in a red skirt,
while Luna wrapped herself in a pink and white floral-print
skirt. Their dark chocolate and caramel-hued skin formed
a blur as they jumped together, held hands, let each other
go, kicked, twirled, spun, bent over to touch their toes, and
carelessly rolled around the floor—getting lint in their hair,
and everything.

In their youthful play, they were teaching us. Educational justice isn't just what happens in the classroom. It's also about the relationships we build as a community to strengthen our capacity to recognize the common thread of humanity in one another. They were reminding us to be free in our expression, to hold each other when we need to, and to let go when we need that too. They were in movement together, connected by a drum that found its way into hymns and dance throughout the African Diaspora and left us with different ways to interpret how we show up in the world.

Finally, when they were done, and all of us were gathering for a group photo, I watched as they gave each other a shared look of satisfaction—an agreement that seemed to confirm that what they had done was meaningful. Embedded in their breaths, now heavier from the play and dance they'd shared, was a discovery of alignment.

Deep breaths in . . .

Deep breaths out.

Deep breaths in . . . a tiny chuckle as the air escaped again.

In their breathing was a reminder that when we honor our shared humanity, we are free to be—not just for ourselves, but also for others who share this journey with us. Our breath makes room for the possibility of freeing ourselves from the narrative of exclusion. It allows us to speak our truths—with all the sass, crass, and boldness we can muster. It allows us to dance—with all of the energy we can conjure.

It allows us to be free.

Acknowledgments

This book was the product of a collective labor and community of support. Extreme gratitude to the women and men who center the wellbeing of Black and Brown girls in their work, lives, and service. Without your creativity, partnership, innovation, commitment, consistency, and love, the examples shared in this book would not have been possible. I would also like to thank the girls, women, and men whose stories are included in this book. You are sacred and loved. Thank you.

I am so grateful for the support of my very large, ever expanding, family—all of you keep me connected to what's real. To my two daughters, Ebony and Mahogany, thank you for choosing me and for offering your talents, wherever you can, in this work to implement the demands of educational justice for girls. To my husband, Greg, writing this book in the midst of your healing journey was no easy task, but your grace, understanding, and patience with my travel schedule was everything. Thank you. #GregStrong.

Massive love to my teachers, beginning with my mother, Katie Couvson, who hung vocabulary plaques and inspirational phrases—in French and English—around our little apartment in San Francisco. I'm still working through the possibility of "knowledge is the goose that laid the golden egg," but I will get there. A shout-out to some special educators over the years: Ms. Penelope, Sister Barbara, Tim Price, Laurie Bottoms, Sudie Sides, Mal Singer, Jackie White, and of course my mentor, Manning Marable. You challenged me and/or gave me the freedom to dream, and it made me better. Lois Loofborrow, you remain the G.O.A.T. for creating a space for me to cultivate possibility. Love you.

I would also like to express gratitude to my funding partners in this work to interrupt school-to-confinement pathways for girls, the NoVo Foundation, Ford Foundation, Stuart Foundation, Ms. Foundation, Communities for Just Schools Fund, Art for Justice Fund, and Schott Foundation for Public Education. I would also like to thank the California Wellness Foundation and the California Endowment for investing in work that specifically helps us create spaces to involve our full communities in the conversation about interrupting school-to-confinement pathways for girls. I would like to extend a special thank you to the Ford Foundation team in Lagos, Nigeria: Innocent Chukwuma, Paul Nwulu, Padma Ugbabe, Dabesaki Mac-Ikemenjima, and Chidinma Ayaku-Nee Ojih; and to the International Institute of Restorative Justice, specifically Keith Hickman and Clarie De Mezerville, for your generosity. Your collective belief in the transformative power of narratives and your willingness to connect me with people making a difference across the globe, make this work so much richer.

The work that provides the foundation of much of my writing is supported by the National Black Women's Justice Institute: Isis Sapp-Grant, Stephanie Bush-Baskette, Aishatu

Yusuf, Falilah Bilal, Ava Montgomery, Andrea Ritchie, Misha Inniss-Thompson, Nicole Kenney, JoHanna Thompson, Dominique Fulling, Dereca Blackmon, and Lesleigh Irish-Underwood. Thank you, NBWJI Board, staff, consultants, and advisors, for being so mighty. Extended thanks to our partners in this work, National Crittenton, The Mentoring Center, Girls, Inc., Alameda County Office of Education, the Georgetown Center on Poverty and Inequality, and every organization—large and small—working to uplift out girls. Education is freedom work! Mary McLeod Bethune knew it. Fannie Barrier Williams knew it. Mary Church Terrell knew it. Daisy Bates knew it. Marva Collins knew it. We know it.

Scholars and artists who examine Black and Brown girlhood and womanhood are the muses for this work. I am inspired by Ntozake Shange, Joyce Ladner, Nikki Giovanni, Maya Angelou, Audre Lorde, Sonia Sanchez, Angela Y. Davis, bell hooks, Celia Cruz, Kimberlé Crenshaw, Priscilla Ocen, ClimbingPoeTree, Brittsense Photography, Jill Scott, Elaine Richardson/Sistah-Scholar, and the emergent scholars and artists who are taking it to the next level. Thank you.

A squad—in my professional and personal life—is essential to maintaining a sense of balance and wellbeing. Thank you, Celsa Snead, Fatima Goss-Graves, Joanne Smith, Rebecca Epstein, Nakisha Lewis, Vivian Anderson, Marcia Rincon-Gallardo, Sara Haskie-Mendoza, Jeannette Pai-Espinosa, Terri Yellow-hammer, Wakumi Douglas, Alisson Brown, Jaime Koppel, Teresa Younger, Jody Myrum, Nzingha Dugas, Antoinnette Davis, Danielle Soto, Ifeoma Udoh, Randa Powell, sujatha baliga, Melissa Harris-Perry, Njema Frazier, Agape Adams, Timothy

McCarthy, Roger Scotland, Denise Pines, Jacoba Atlas, Erika Brown, Susan Burton, and of course, my sorors of Delta Sigma Theta Sorority, Inc. You all encourage me to continue centering the unconditional positive question about how we effectively counter the criminalization of our youth. I learn from you, and we will do this.

To my literary agent, Marie Brown, you already know how much I love and appreciate your wisdom and insights. Thank you for "feeling me" through this. To my editor, Tara Grove, you also know how lucky I feel to work with you and The New Press on this body of work. Your attention to detail and support for my voice in this public discourse is a blessing.

To Prince Rogers Nelson, thank you for gifting us with "Anna Stesia" and a lifetime of music to explore the unconditional healing power of love.

Finally, to the blues women whose wisdom informed the core learnings and teachings in this work, thank you. Generations later, we see you. We honor you.

Notes

Epigraph

Angela Y. Davis, *Are Prisons Obsolete?* (New York: Seven Stories Press, 2003), 108.

Introduction: Blue Moments

1. Lorin Eleni Gill and Olga R. Rodriguez, "DA: 'My Heart Is Broken' for Subway Stabbing Victims' Family," Associated Press, July 25, 2018; and Michelle Toy and Elissa Harrington, "27-Year-Old Man Sought in Deadly Stabbing at BART Station," KTVU.com, July 23, 2018.

2. #SayHerName raises awareness of the persistent public and private violence against Black women and girls. The movement seeks to combat the erasure of Black women in public discourses about violence and safety, particularly in association with (but not limited to) police violence. See Kimberlé Crenshaw and Andrea Ritchie, *#SayHerName: Resisting Police Brutality Against Black Women*, African American Policy Forum, 2015.

3. Angela Y. Davis, *Blues Legacies and Black Feminism: Gertrude "Ma" Rainey, Bessie Smith, and Billie Holiday* (New York: Vintage Books, 1998), 196–97.

4. Audre Lorde, "The Uses of Anger: Women Responding to Racism," *Women's Studies Quarterly*, City University of New York, Fall 1981.

Track 1: Fit to Wear a Crown

1. Columbus City Preparatory School for Girls, a middle school in Central Ohio, has a student population that is 82 percent Black, 6 percent Hispanic, and 4 percent two or more races. In this school, 86 percent of the students are from low-income families, and the student-to-teacher ratio is 22:1. See https://www.greatschools.org/ohio/columbus/9782-Columbus-City-Preparatory-School-For-Girls/#Students.

2. Nationwide, 2.7 million students in grades K–12, or 5–6 percent of the total student population, were suspended in 2015–16. Black girls represent 8 percent of all students enrolled in public schools, but are 14 percent of those experiencing out-of-school suspension. At nearly seven times greater than their white counterparts, African American girls experience the greatest racial disparity in out-of-school suspensions (OSSes). Black girls are 16 percent of girls in public schools, but they represent 28 percent of girls restrained in schools, 37 percent of girls suspended, and 55 percent of girls experiencing out-of-school suspensions. Among charter schools that report data on suspensions and expulsions, African American girls represent about 29 percent of the student population, but are 70 percent of girls experiencing one or more OSSes and 54 percent of girls experiencing one or more ISS. Per the U.S. Department of Education Office for Civil Rights, restraint is being placed in seclusion or involuntary confinement or being physically restrained completely or partially. Latinx students are not reported to experience an overrepresentation nationwide, but in elementary schools, Latina students comprise 40 percent of arrests among girls, a rate three times higher than that of their white counterparts. See U.S. Department of Education, Office for Civil Rights, *2015–16 Civil Rights Data Collection, School Climate and Safety*, April 2018, p. 13; and Misha N. Innis-Thompson, *Summary of Discipline Data for Girls in U.S. Public Schools* (NBWJI Data Sheet on School Discipline and Girls of Color) (Berkeley, CA: National Black Women's Justice Institute, October 2018).

3. Monique W. Morris, *Pushout: The Criminalization of Black Girls in Schools* (New York: The New Press, 2016).

4. Edward W. Morris and Brea L. Perry, "Girls Behaving Badly? Race, Gender, and Subjective Evaluation in the Discipline of African American Girls," *Sociology of Education* 90, no. 2 (February 2017): 127–48.

5. Morris and Perry, "Girls Behaving Badly?," 144.

6. Gordon A. Crews and M. Reid Counts, *The Evolution of School Disturbance in America: Colonial Times to Modern Day* (Westport, CT: Praeger, 1997), 3.

7. Robert Freeman Butts and Lawrence Arthur Cremin, *A History of Education in American Culture* (New York: Holt, Rinehart & Winston, 1953).

8. American Civil Liberties Union, *Kenny v. Wilson*, March 16, 2017, www.aclu.org/cases/kenny-v-wilson.

9. Natalie Martinez, "'They Hurted': Mom Says Daughter Put in Handcuffs at School," NBCChicago.com, March 18, 2016.

10. Albert Einstein, *Out of My Later Years*, rev. ed. (New York: Citadel Press, 1956, 1984), 33.

11. Joan L. Curcio and Patricia F. First, *Violence in the Schools: How to Proactively Prevent and Defuse It* (Newbury Park, CA: Sage Publications, 1993); and Amity L. Noltemeyer and Rose Marie Ward, "Relationship Between School Suspension and Student Outcomes: A Meta-Analysis," *School Psychology Review* 44, no. 2 (June 2015): 224–40.

12. Libby Nelson and Dara Lind, "The School to Prison Pipeline, Explained," Justice Policy Institute, February 24, 2015, http://www.justicepolicy.org/news/8775.

13. Lawrence M. DeRidder, "The Impact of School Suspensions and Expulsions on Dropping Out," *Educational Horizons* 68, no. 3, Administrative Evaluation (Spring 1990): 153—57; and Noltemeyer, Ward, and Mcloughlin, "Relationship Between School Suspension and Student Outcomes," 224–40.

14. Russ Skiba and Reece Peterson, "The Dark Side of Zero Tolerance: Can Punishment Lead to Safe Schools?" *Phi Delta Kappan* 80, no. 5 (January 1999): 372–76, 381–82.

15. Zaretta Hammond, *Culturally Responsive Teaching and the Brain: Promoting Authentic Engagement and Rigor Among Culturally and Linguistically Diverse Students* (Thousand Oaks, CA: Corwin/Sage, 2015), 45.

16. Harvard University Center on the Developing Child, Key Concepts, "Toxic Stress," developingchild.harvard.edu/science/key-concepts/toxic-stress.

17. Vincent Felitti et al., "Relationship of Childhood Abuse and Household Dysfunction to Many of the Leading Causes of Death in Adults: The Adverse Childhood Experiences (ACE) Study," *American Journal of Preventative Medicine* 14, no. 4 (May 1998): 245–58.

18. Audre Lorde, "The Master's Tools Will Never Dismantle Master's House," from *Sister Outsider*, Crossing Press Feminist Series (1979, 1984 ed.).

19. Erica Green and Katie Benner, "Louisiana School Made Headlines for Sending Black Kids to Elite Colleges: Here's the Reality," *New York Times*, November 30, 2018.

20. Crews and Counts, *The Evolution of School Disturbance in America*, 4.

21. American Institute for Research, "School Discipline Laws & Regulations by Category," National Center on Safe Supportive Learning Environments (Washington, DC: U.S. Department of Education Office of Safe and Healthy Students), safesupportivelearning.ed.gov/node/3510; and Jess Clark, "Where Corporal Punishment Is Still Used In Schools, Its Roots Run Deep," NPR.org, April 17, 2017.

22. Elizabeth Gershoff and Sarah Font, "Corporal Punishment in U.S. Public Schools: Prevalence, Disparities in Use, and Status in State and Federal Policy," Society for Research in Social Development, *Social Policy Report* 30, no. 1 (September 2016).

23. Clifton P. Flynn, "Regional Differences in Attitudes Toward Corporal Punishment," *Journal of Marriage and Family* 56, no. 2 (May 1994): 314–24, doi:10.2307/353102.

24. Gershoff and Font, "Corporal Punishment." See also Elizabeth T. Gershoff, Kelly M. Purtell, and Igor Holas, *Corporal Punishment in U.S. Public Schools: Legal Precedents, Current Practices, and Future Policy*, Springer Briefs in Psychology Series, Advances in Child and Family Policy and Practice Subseries (New York: Springer, 2015).

25. United Nations Convention on the Rights of the Child:

> Article 19, 1. States Parties shall take all appropriate legislative, administrative, social and educational measures to protect the child from all forms of physical or mental violence, injury or abuse, neglect or negligent treatment, maltreatment or exploitation, including sexual abuse, while in the care of parent(s), legal guardian(s) or any other person who has the care of the child. . . .

> Article 28, 2. States Parties shall take all appropriate measures to ensure that school discipline is administered in a manner consistent with the child's human dignity and in conformity with the present Convention.

> Article 37. States Parties shall ensure that: (a) No child shall be subjected to torture or other cruel, inhuman or degrading treatment or punishment. Neither capital punishment nor life imprisonment without possibility of release shall be imposed for offences committed by persons below eighteen years of age. . . .

26. Analysis by National Black Women's Justice Institute of data from U.S. Department of Education Office for Civil Rights, 2018.

27. Crews and Counts, *Evolution of School Disturbance*. According to psychologist Stacy Patton, "Historians and anthropologists have found no evidence that ritualistic forms of physical discipline of children existed in precolonial West African societies prior to the Atlantic slave trade. West African societies held children in a much higher regard than slave societies in the Atlantic world, which placed emphasis on black bodies as property, not as human beings. West Africans believed that children came from the afterlife, that they were gods or reincarnated ancestors who led profoundly spiritual lives and held extraordinary mystical powers that

could be harnessed through ritual practice for the good of the community." Stacy Patton, "Corporal Punishment in Black Communities: Not an Intrinsic Cultural Tradition but Racial Trauma," *Children, Youth and Family News*, American Psychological Association, April 2017.

28. Albert Bandura proposes that behavior is a function of observation, imitation, and interactions/modeling. Children learn how to behave by experiencing responses from adults (and other children), from observing the consequences associated with the behavior of others in their environments, and by using cognitive processes to determine or mediate behaviors toward the development of personal agency. See Albert Bandura, *Social Learning Theory* (Englewood Cliffs, NJ: Prentice Hall, 1977), and *Social Foundations of Thought and Action: A Social Cognitive Theory* (Prentice-Hall, 1986).

29. Phoebe S. Moore, Shannon E. Whaley, and Marian Sigman, "Interactions Between Mothers and Children: Impacts of Maternal and Child Anxiety," *Journal of Abnormal Psychology* 113, no. 3 (August 2004): 471–76; and Patrick T. Davies et al., "Child Emotional Security and Interparental Conflict," *Monographs of the Society for Research in Child Development* 67, no. 3 (2002), www.jstor/org/stable/3181513.

30. Rebekah Levine Coley, Melissa A. Kull, and Jennifer Carrano, "Parental Endorsement of Spanking and Children's Internalizing and Externalizing Problems in African-American and Hispanic Families," *Journal of Family Psychology* 28, no. 1 (February 2014): 22–31.

31. Murray A. Straus and Glenda Kaufman Kantor, "Corporal Punishment of Adolescents by Parents: A Risk Factor in the Epidemiology of Depression." *Adolescence* [serial online] 29, no. 115 (Fall 1994): 543, available from SPORTDiscus with Full Text, www.ebsco.com/products/research-databases/sportdiscus-full-text.

32. Akemi Tomoda et al., "Reduced Prefrontal Cortical Gray Matter Volume in Young Adults Exposed to Harsh Corporal Punishment," *NeuroImage* 47, Supplement 2 (August 2009): T66–T71; see also David M.

Amodio and Chris D. Frith, "Meeting of Minds: The Medial Frontal Cortex and Social Cognition," *Nature Reviews Neuroscience* 7, no. 4 (April 2006): 268–77.

33. Tomoda et al., "Reduced Prefrontal Cortical Gray Matter Volume."

34. Paolo Friere. *Pedagogy of the Oppressed* (London: Continuum International Publishing Group, 1970, 1993), 48–49.

35. Paulo Freire, *Pedagogy of the Oppressed*, trans. Myra Bergman Ramos (London: Continuum, 2000), 74.

Track 2: God Bless the Child That's Got Her Own

1. Vincent Felitti et al., "Relationship of Childhood Abuse and Household Dysfunction to Many of the Leading Causes of Death in Adults: The Adverse Childhood Experiences."

2. Nadine Burke-Harris, *The Deepest Well: Healing the Long-Term Effects of Childhood Adversity* (Boston: Houghton Mifflin Harcourt, 2018), 66.

3. Burke-Harris, *Deepest Well*, 20.

4. Burke-Harris, *Deepest Well*, 155–72.

5. Helen Y. Weng et al., "Compassion Training Alters Altruism and Neural Responses to Suffering," *Psychological Science* 24, no. 7 (July 2013), 1171–80.

6. Association for Psychological Science, "Brain Can Be Trained in Compassion, Study Shows," press release, May 22, 2013.

7. Rebecca Epstein, Jamilia Blake, and Thalia González, *Girlhood Interrupted: The Erasure of Black Girls' Childhood* (Washington, DC: Georgetown Center on Poverty and Inequality, 2017), 1.

8. Epstein et al., *Girlhood Interrupted*, 7.

9. Epstein et al., *Girlhood Interrupted*, 8.

10. Child Mind Institute, "Signs of Trauma in Children: What to Watch for in the Weeks and Months After an Upsetting Event," https://childmind.org/article/signs-trauma-children.

11. Debora L. Roorda et al., "The Influence of Affective Teacher-Student Relationships on Students' School Engagement and Achievement: A Meta-analytic Approach," *Review of Educational Research* 81, no. 4 (December 2011): 493–529, doi: 10.3102/0034654311421793.

12. Jason Okonofua, David Paunesku, and Gregory Walton, "Brief Intervention to Encourage Empathic Discipline Cuts Suspension Rates in Half Among Adolescents," *Proceedings of the National Academy of Sciences* 113, no. 19 (May 10, 2016): 5221–26.

13. Okonofua et al., "Brief Intervention," 5224.

14. Okonofua et al., "Brief Intervention," 5222.

15. Brittany Brathwaite, excerpt from comments for a webinar hosted by the National Black Women's Justice Institute on Policing in Schools, April 13, 2018.

16. Amy Brown, "Waiting for Superwoman: White Female Teachers and the Construction of the 'Neoliberal Savior' in a New York City Public School," *Journal for Critical Education Policy Studies* 11, no. 2 (March 2013): 124–60.

17. Teach for Nigeria, www.teachfornigeria.com.

18. Joy DeGruy, *Post-traumatic Slave Syndrome* (self-published, 2005, ebook), loc. 1536, 4133.

19. Christopher Emdin, *For White Folks Who Teach in the Hood, and the Rest of Yall Too: Reality Pedagogy and Urban Education* (Boston: Beacon Press, 2016), 27.

20. Tammerlin Drummond, "Black Panther School a Legend in Its Time," *East Bay Times* (Walnut Creek, CA), October 28, 2016.

21. Race Forward: The Center for Racial Justice Innovation (formerly Applied Research Center), "Racial Equity Impact Assessment" and "Racial Equity Impact Assessment Toolkit," www.RaceForward.org, Oakland, CA.

22. Lexa Dundore, "Food System Racial Equity Assessment Tool: A Facilitation Guide," University of Wisconsin Cooperative Extension, Madison, learningstore.uwex.edu/Assets/pdfs/G4134.pdf.

23. Jonathan Cohen, "Social, Emotional, Ethical, and Academic Education: Creating a Climate for Learning, Participation in Democracy, and Well-Being," *Harvard Educational Review* 76, no. 2 (Summer 2006): 201–85, at 202.

24. Jonathan Cohen, "Social, Emotional," 208–9.

25. Niroga Institute, "What Is Dynamic Mindfulness?" DMind.org, 2018.

26. Deepak Chopra, *Living in Awareness,* The Chopra Center, https://chopra.com/online-courses/living-in-awareness/on-demand.

27. Deborah Bloom, "Instead of Detention, These Students Get Meditation," CNN.com, November 8, 2016, https://www.cnn.com/2016/11/04/health/meditation-in-schools-baltimore/index.html.

28. Kimberly A. Schonert-Reichl, Eva Oberle, Molly Stewart Lawlor, David Abbott, Kimberly Thomson, Tim F. Oberlander, and Adele Diamond, "Enhancing Cognitive and Social–Emotional Development Through a Simple-to-Administer Mindfulness-Based School Program for Elementary School Children: A Randomized Controlled Trial," *Developmental Psychology* 51, no. 1 (2015), 52–66.

29. Priscilla Dass-Brailsford, *A Practical Approach to Trauma: Empowering Interventions* (Los Angeles: Sage, 2007). See also, and see also Kimberly Frazier, Cirecie A. West-Olatunji, Shirley St. Juste, and Rachael D. Goodman, "Transgenerational Trauma and Child Sexual Abuse: Reconceptualizing Cases Involving Young Survivors of CSA," *Journal of Mental Health Counseling* 31, no. 1 (January 2009), 22–33.

30. Gayle Flynn, *Investigating Relational Aggression and Bullying for Girls' of Color in Oklahoma: A Phenomenological Study,* Dissertation, Liberty University (2016), 123–32.

31. Lillian Comas-Díaz and Beverly Greene, "Culturally Competent Psychological Interventions with Women of Color," *Psychological Health of Women of Color: Intersections, Challenges, and Opportunities* (Westport, CT: Praeger, 2013), 375.

32. Comas-Díaz and Greene, "Culturally Competent Psychological Interventions," 376.

33. Joy DeGruy, *Post-traumatic Slave Syndrome* (self-published, 2005, ebook).

34. Monique W. Morris, "Sacred Inquiry and Delinquent Black Girls: Developing a Foundation for a Liberative Pedagogical Praxis," in G. D. Sardana and Tojo Thatchenkery, eds., *Understanding Work Experiences from Multiple Perspectives: New Paradigms for Organizational Excellence* (New Delhi: Bloomsbury India, 2015), 418.

35. Ebony White, "Trauma in the Classroom: Introducing a New Strategy for Teachers." *Phillis, The Journal for Research on African American Women* 4, no. 1 (2016–17). Information about DTEC may be accessed here: https://www.dtecteacheracademy.com.

36. The Trauma Informed Schools Learning Network for Girls of Color is operated by the Georgetown Center on Poverty and Inequality and the National Black Women's Justice Institute for educators and adults working in schools. Educators may register here: http://schools4girlsofcolor.org/apply.

Track 3: Cell Bound Blues

1. Monique Morris, Rebecca Epstein, and Aishatu Yusuf, *Be Her Resource: A Toolkit About School Resource Officers and Girls of Color* (Washington, DC: Georgetown Law Center on Poverty and Inequality, September 2017), 24.

2. Kimberlé Crenshaw and Andrea Ritchie, *#SayHerName: Resisting Police Brutality Against Black Women*, African American Policy Forum, 2015; and Andrea Ritchie, *Invisible No More: Police Violence Against Black Women and Women of Color* (New York: Beacon Press, 2017).

3. Ritchie, *Invisible No More.*

4. National Association of School Resource Officers, NASRO.org /about.

5. U.S. Department of Education and U.S. Department of Justice, Office of Justice Programs, *Indicators of School Crime and Safety: 2017* (March 2018), 10.

6. Lucinda Gray, Laurie Lewis, and John Ralph, *Public School Safety and Discipline: 2013-14, First Look*, U.S. Department of Education, National Center on Education Statistics, 11 (May 2015), 11.

7. According to the U.S. Department of Education National Center on Education Statistics, 75 percent of all public schools have security cameras and 43 percent have security guards, security personnel, school resource officers, or other sworn law enforcement officers on campus. See Gray, Lewis, and Ralph, *Public School Safety*, 10.

8. Law enforcement is more likely to participate in noncriminalizing activities with students, such as identifying problems and proactively seeking solutions (90 percent), training teachers and staff in school safety and crime prevention (64 percent), and teaching law-related education courses for students (54 percent). By comparison, in schools where less than half of the student population is white, only 45 percent of law enforcement train teachers or staff in school safety and crime prevention, and only 21 percent teach law-related courses for students. See Gray, Lewis, and Ralph, *Public School Safety*, 13.

9. Black girls are 37 percent of girls arrested in school, and 43 percent of girls referred to law enforcement. Latina students, who are 25 percent of the female student population nationwide, disproportionately experience referrals to law enforcement (33 percent). Latina students are 40 percent of girls experiencing elementary school arrests, and are three times more likely than their white counterparts at that age to be arrested. Overall, African American girls are twice as likely to experience an arrest on campus as their white counterparts.

10. Advancement Project, Dignity in Schools Campaign, NAACP Legal Defense and Education Fund, Inc., and the Alliance for Educational Justice, *Police in Schools Are Not the Answer to School Shootings*. Re-released March 2018.

11. Ben Brown and William Reed Benedict, "Perceptions of the Police: Past Findings, Methodological Issues, Conceptual Issues, and Policy Implications," *Policing* 25, no. 3 (September 2002): 543–80. See also, Scott H. Decker, "Citizen Attitudes Toward the Police: A Review of Past Findings and Suggestions for Future Policy," *Journal of Police Science and Administration*, 9, no. 1 (March 1981): 80–87.

12. Arrick Jackson, "Police School Resource Officers' and Students' Perception of the Police and Offending," *Policing* 25, no. 3 (September 2002): 631–50. See also Brown and Benedict, "Perceptions of the Police"; and "Classroom Cops: What Do the Students Think? A Case Study of Student Perceptions of School Police and Security Officers Conducted in an Hispanic Community," *International Journal of Police Science and Management* 7 no. 4 (December 2005): 280.

13. Jackson, "Police School Resource," 648.

14. Aaron Sussman, "Learning in Lockdown: School Police, Race, and the Limits of the Law, *UCLA Law Review* 59 (February 2012): 788–849, at 803.

15. Steve Pickett, "DISD Officer Off Duty After Taking Down 6th Grader," CBS DFW (Dallas–Fort Worth), May 16, 2017.

16. Jessica Schladebeck, "Police Officer Captured on Video Body Slamming 12-Year-Old Girl in Dallas School," *New York Daily News*, May 16, 2017.

17. Morris, Epstein, and Yusuf, *Be Her Resource*, 25.

18. Darnell Felix Hawkins, "Devalued Lives and Racial Stereotypes: Ideological Barriers to the Prevention of Family Violence Among Blacks," in Robert L. Hampton, ed., *Violence in the Black Family* (San Francisco: Jossey-Bass, 2006), 189–206.

19. Monique Williams and Isis Sapp-Grant, "From Punishment to Rehabilitation: Empowering African American Youths," *Souls: A Critical Journal of Black Politics, Culture, and Society* 2, no. 1 (Winter 2000): 55–60.

20. Discipline data for parochial and independent schools are not publicly available in a disaggregated manner. However, private schools most often utilize a code of conduct contract with students and parents delineating consequences of misconduct. These vary and the data are not publicly available. Anecdotes from students and alumnae of private schools describe differential treatment such as being accused of not paying for lunch when they did. The student composition of most private schools remain non-Black/Latinx/Indigenous, which may facilitate marginalization through blatant racism, microaggressions, adultification, or worse. See Arah Iloabugichukwu, "Not Every Black Girl Survives Private School," MadameNoire.com, December 10, 2018. See also, Leah Thomas, "My Private School Experience as a Black Liberal," HuffingtonPost.com, January 3, 2017, and the Schott Foundation for Public Education, "The War on Black Girls' Hair in Private and Charter Schools," May 19, 2017, http://schottfoundation.org/blog/2017/05/19/war-black-girls-hair-private-and-charter-schools.

21. Dorothy Roberts, *Killing the Black Body: Race, Reproduction, and the Meaning of Liberty* (New York: Vintage Books, 1998), 19.

22. Jason Hanna, "This Wounded Parkland Student Won't Return to Her High School: But She'll Still Get Her Diploma," CNN.com, February 28, 2018.

23. Moriah Balingit, "Trump's Solution for School Shootings: Arm Teachers, Post Veterans with Guns," *Chicago Tribune*, February 21, 2018.

24. Anne Branigin, "Black Students at Stoneman Douglas High Want Gun-Violence Solutions to Address Police Violence," TheRoot.com, March 29, 2018.

25. Sheryl Kataoka et al., "Responding to students with posttraumatic stress disorder in schools," *Child and adolescent psychiatric clinics of North America,* vol. 21, 1 (2012): 119–33, x. See also Michelle Bosquet, "How research informs clinical work with traumatized young children," 301–25 in J. Osofsky, ed., *Young Children and Trauma: Intervention and Treatment* (New York: Guildford Press, 2007), and see also Eliana Gil, "Helping abused and traumatized children: Integrating directive and nondirective approaches" (New York: Guilford Press, 2006).

26. Shanifa Nasser, "Canada's Largest School Board Votes to End Armed Police Presence in Schools," CBC News, November 22, 2017.

27. Stephen Nathan Haymes, *Race, Culture, and the City: A Pedagogy for Black Urban Struggle* (Albany: State University of New York Press, 1995), 145.

Track 4: Nobody Knows My Name

1. Lauren Morando Rhim, Jessica Sutter, and Neil Campbell, "Improving Outcomes for Students with Disabilities: Negotiating Common Ground for District and Charter School Collaboration," Center for American Progress, Washington, DC, January 31, 2017.

2. Black girls were 18 percent of girls served in schools under the Individuals with Disabilities Education Act (IDEA), but 45 percent of girls with disabilities receiving at least one OSS, 34 percent of girls with disabilities receiving at least one ISS, 48 percent of girls with disabilities arrested on campus, and 31 percent of girls with disabilities referred to law enforcement. See Misha N. Inniss-Thompson, *Prevalence of Discipline Practices for Female Students with Disabilities Served Under IDEA: An Analysis of 2013–14 U.S. Department of Education Office for Civil Rights Data Collection,* National Black Women's Justice Institute, November 2017.

3. At the time of my presentation, African American girls were four times more likely than white girls with disabilities to receive an OSS, three times more likely to be arrested, two and a half times more likely

to be referred to law enforcement, and twice as likely to receive an ISS. Latina students were almost twice as likely as their white counterparts to be arrested in schools. See Inniss-Thompson, *Prevalence of Discipline Practices*.

4. Jamila Codrington and Halford H. Fairchild, *Special Education and the Miseducation of African American Children: A Call to Action*, position paper, Association of Black Psychologists, Washington, DC.

5. Moriah Balingit, "DeVos Rescinds 72 Guidance Documents Outlining Rights for Students With Disabilities," *Chicago Tribune*, October 21, 2017; and Daniella Silva, "Betsy DeVos Overhauls Obama-Era Title IX Guidance on Campus Sex Assault," NBC News, September 7, 2017.

6. Sandra T., "Sexual Abuse and Power: Disabled Black Girls' Positions in the World," Mamablack.com, August 10, 2016.

7. National Women's Law Center, *How to Protect Students from Sexual Harassment: A Primer for Schools*, 2007.

8. sujatha baliga, "A Different Path for Confronting Sexual Assault: What Is Restorative Justice? A Practitioner Explains How It Works," *Vox*, October 10, 2018.

9. Khadija Hudson and Brittany Brathwaite, *The Schools Girls Deserve: Youth-Driven Solutions for Creating Safe, Holistic, and Affirming New York City Public Schools* (New York: Girls for Gender Equity, 2017), 15.

10. Hudson and Brathwaite, *Schools Girls Deserve*, 12.

11. Hudson and Brathwaite, *Schools Girls Deserve*, 28.

12. Andrea Ritchie, *Expanding Our Frame: Deepening Our Demands for Safety and Healing for Black Survivors of Sexual Violence*, National Black Women's Justice Institute and the Ms. Foundation for Safety (2019), 14.

13. Ritchie, *Expanding Our Frame*, 15.

14. National Institute on Drug Abuse, "Principles of Adolescent Substance Use Disorder Treatment: A Research-Based Guide," www.DrugAbuse.gov, January 2014.

15. Kenneth W. Griffin and Gilbert J. Botvin, "Evidence-based interventions for preventing substance use disorders in adolescents," *Child and Adolescent Psychiatric Clinics of North America*, vol. 19, 3 (2010): 505–26.

16. Ronald Dahl et al., "Importance of Investing in Adolescence from a Developmental Science Perspective," *Nature* 554, no. 7693 (February 22, 2018): 441–50, at 446.

17. Charlotte Jacobs, "Developing the 'Oppositional Gaze': Using Critical Media Pedagogy and Black Feminist Thought to Promote Black Girls' Identity Development," *Journal of Negro Education* 85, no. 3 (July 2016): 225–38, at 226.

18. Gary W. Kuhne and Allan B. Quigley, "Understanding and Using Action Research in Practice Settings," *New Directions in Adult and Continuing Education*, no. 73 (Spring 1997): 23–39.

19. Monique W. Morris, "Sacred Inquiry and Delinquent Black Girls: Developing a Foundation for a Liberative Pedagogical Praxis," in Sardana and Thatchenkery, eds., *Understanding Work Experiences.*

20. Jacobs, "Developing the 'Oppositional Gaze,'" 230.

21. Jennifer Esposito and Erica Edwards, "When Black Girls Fight: Interrogating, Interrupting, and (Re)Imagining Dangerous Scripts of Femininity in Urban Classrooms," *Education and Urban Society* 50, no. 4 (September 2017): 87–107; see also, Detra Price-Dennis, "Developing Curriculum to Support Black Girls' Literacies in Digital Spaces," *English Education* 48, no. 4 (July 2016), 337–61.

22. Candice Aston et al., "Promoting Sisterhood: The Impact of a Culturally Focused Program to Address Verbally Aggressive Behaviors in Black Girls," *Psychology in the Schools* 55, no. 1 (December 2017): 50–62.

23. Vera López and Meda Chesney-Lind, "Latina Girls Speak Out: Stereotypes, Gender and Relationship Dynamics," *Latino Studies*, vol. 12, 4, 527–49, www.palgrave-journals.com/lst/.

24. Dominique C. Hill, "Black Girl Pedagogies: Layered Lessons on Reliability," *Curriculum Inquiry* 48, no. 1 (July 2018): 383–405.

25. Jeremiah L. Young, Marquita D. Foster, and Dorothy Hines, "Even Cinderella Is White: (Re)Centering Black Girls' Voices as Literacies of Resistance," *English Journal* 107, no. 6 (July 2018): 102–8.

26. Simone Gibson, "Adolescent African American Girls as Engaged Readers: Challenging Stereotypical Images of Black Womanhood Through Urban Fiction," *Journal of Negro Education* 85, no. 3 (Summer 2016): 212–24; see also Nia Michelle Nunn, "Super-Girl: Strength and Sadness in Black Girlhood, *Gender and Education* 30, no. 2 (September 2016): 239–58.

27. Heather Stuckey and Jeremy Nobel, "The Connection Between Art, Healing, and Public Health: A Review of Current Literature," *American Journal of Public Health* 100, no. 2 (February 2010): 254–63, at 255.

28. Stuckey and Nobel, "The Connection," 257, 259–60. Specifically, visual arts have been demonstrated to help women "focus on positive life experiences," find "enhanced self-worth and identity," "maintain a social identity" outside of their illness or condition, and provided an opportunity for women to use symbols to express feelings. Dance, theater, and other creative movement have been associated with supporting self-awareness and "gains on both cognitive and psychological well-being measures, [specifically] word and listening recall, problem-solving, self-esteem, and psychological well-being" (259). Creative writing improves physical health, immune system functioning, control over pain and depression, psychological well-being, and resistance to fatigue. Journal writing has been particularly effective, in elevating "creativity, spiritual awareness, and expansion of the self" (259–60).

29. Nunn, "Super-Girl," 240.

30. This original poem is composed from a collection of "call me" requests from girls of color participating in a meeting in Portland, Oregon, in the summer of 2018. Girls and young women who participated in this meeting were ages fourteen to twenty-one and hailed from Washington, California, Kansas, Colorado, New York, Mississippi, and Oregon.

Track 5: Shake Hands with the Devil, Make Him Crawl in the Sand

1. Restorative Practices Consortium, International Institute of Restorative Practices, Ontario, Canada.

2. Open Society Institute, *Baltimore City Public Schools Restorative Practices Report* (2017), 29.

3. Matthew Fanselow and Donella Bellett, *Evaluation of Restorative Practice: A Positive Behaviour for Learning Programme*, Ministry of Education, New Zealand (May 31, 2018), https://www.educationcounts.govt.nz/__data/assets/pdf_file/0010/185752/PB4L-Evaluation-of-restorative-practice2.pdf.

4. See Centre for Justice and Reconciliation, Prison Fellowship International. http://restorativejustice.org/restorative-justice/about-restorative-justice/around-the-world/#sthash.S6uarti3.dpbs.

5. See David Washburn and Daniel Willis, "The rise of restorative justice in California schools brings promise, controversy," EdSource. https://edsource.org/2018/the-rise-of-restorative-justice-in-california-schools-brings-promise-controversy/597393. See also, the Restorative Justice Initiative, http://www.restorativejustice.nyc; and the International Institute of Restorative Practices, https://www.iirp.edu.

6. Trevor Fronius et al., *Restorative Justice in U.S. Schools: A Research Review* (San Francisco: WestEd Justice and Prevention Research Center, February 2016).

7. Fronius et al., *Restorative Justice*, 12–13.

8. For more information, see Kay Pranis, "The Restorative Impulse," *Tikkun* 27, no. 1 (Winter 2012): 33–34.

9. Elaine Richardson, "My Ill-Literacy Narrative: Growing Up Black, Po and a Girl, in the Hood," *Gender and Education* 21, no. 6 (November 2009): 753–67.

10. Interview with Celsa Snead, executive director of the Mentoring Center, 2018.

11. Davis, *Are Prisons Obsolete?*, 108.

Track 6: "Today I'm with You . . . Ain't That Some Love"

1. Michael G. Vaughn et al., "Childhood Reports of Food Neglect and Impulse Control Problems and Violence in Adulthood," *International Journal of Environmental Research and Public Health* 13, no. 4 (March 2016), 389.

2. Susan Popkin, Molly Scott, and Martha Galvez, *Impossible Choices: Teens and Food Insecurity in America* (Washington, DC: Urban Institute, 2016).

3. Louise Ivers and Kimberly Cullen, "Food Insecurity: Special Considerations for Women," *American Journal of Clinical Nutrition* 94, no. 6 (December 2011): 1740S–1744S.

4. Free and Reduced-Price Lunch is used as a proxy for student poverty. Seventy-four percent of Black students attend mid-high to high poverty schools and are eligible to receive free and reduced-price lunches (FRPL) in U.S. public schools; 73 percent of Latinx/Hispanic students attend mid-high to high poverty schools; and 67 percent of Indigenous (American Indian/Alaskan Native) students attend mid-high to high poverty schools. See U.S. Department of Education, National Center for Education Statistics (2018), *The Condition of Education 2018* (NCES 2018, 144), Concentration of Public School Students Eligible for Free or Reduced-Price Lunch.

5. Blessings in a Backpack's mission is to "mobilize communities, individuals and resources to provide food on the weekends for elementary school children across America who might otherwise go hungry"; see https://www.blessingsinabackpack.org.

6. According to Feeding America, "For more than 15 years, the Feeding America BackPack Program has been helping children get the nutritious

and easy-to-prepare food they need to get enough to eat on the weekends";
see www.feedingamerica.org/our-work/hunger-relief-programs/backpack
-program.

7. Kids Gardening: kidsgardening.org/what-we-do.

8. NAACP National Website, www.naacp.org/issues/civicengagement.

9. UniDosUS, 2017 Annual Report.

10. National Black Women's Justice Institute and Boston City-Councilor At-Large Ayanna Pressley. *Project Focus: School Culture and Discipline Reform in Boston-Area Primary and Secondary Schools, Policy Recommendations* (March 2018).

11. Freire, *Pedagogy of the Oppressed*, 109.

Coda

1. Nikki Giovanni, "Revolutionary Dreams," in *The Women and the Men: Poems* (New York: Morrow, 1975).

About the Author

Monique W. Morris, Ed.D., co-founder of the National Black Women's Justice Institute, is the author of several books, including *Pushout* and *Black Stats* (both from The New Press). Her work has been featured by NPR, the *New York Times*, MSNBC, *Essence*, *The Atlantic*, TED, the *Washington Post*, *Education Week*, and others. She lives in the Bay Area with her husband and two daughters.

Publishing in the Public Interest

Thank you for reading this book published by The New Press. The New Press is a nonprofit, public interest publisher. New Press books and authors play a crucial role in sparking conversations about the key political and social issues of our day.

We hope you enjoyed this book and that you will stay in touch with The New Press. Here are a few ways to stay up to date with our books, events, and the issues we cover:

- Sign up at www.thenewpress.com/subscribe to receive updates on New Press authors and issues and to be notified about local events
- Like us on Facebook: www.facebook.com/newpressbooks
- Follow us on Twitter: www.twitter.com/thenewpress

Please consider buying New Press books for yourself; for friends and family; or to donate to schools, libraries, community centers, prison libraries, and other organizations involved with the issues our authors write about.

The New Press is a 501(c)(3) nonprofit organization. You can also support our work with a tax-deductible gift by visiting www.thenewpress.com/donate.